LIVING
WITH
PLANTS

LIVING
WITH
PLANTS

GEORGE CARTER

PHOTOGRAPHY BY MARIANNE MAJERUS

MITCHELL BEAZLEY

LIVING WITH PLANTS
by George Carter

First published in Great Britain in 2000 by Mitchell Beazley,
an imprint of Octopus Publishing Group Ltd, 2–4 Heron Quays,
London E14 4JP

Copyright © Octopus Publishing Group Ltd 2000

Executive Editors **Alison Starling and Mark Fletcher**
Executive Art Editor **Vivienne Brar**
Editors **Selina Mumford and Penny Warren**
Designers **Lovelock & Co., Helen Taylor and Vicky Short**
Picture Research **Claire Gouldstone**
Production **Nancy Roberts**
Proof reader **Laura Hicks**
Index **Sue Farr**

ISBN 1 84000 181 X

A CIP record for this book is available from the British Library

Set in Stone Sans

Colour reproduction by ERAY SCAN PTE LTD, Singapore
Produced by Toppan Printing Co., (HK) Ltd.
Printed and bound in China

CONTENTS

INTRODUCTION

House plants have been an important element in interior decoration for many centuries, but their status and function has changed with each generation. A great deal of fun is to be had from ransacking history for ideas – not just in order to reconstruct 'period' effects, but because most of the best planting ideas have already been formulated and are readily adaptable to modern conditions. Sometimes plants were present in the home for functional or symbolic reasons (see below) or as a collection of curiosities and rarities (see right), but often they have been the inspiration for and the major element in an entire decorative scheme (see below right).

One might think that the blurring of the distinction between indoors and out, between house and garden, is a product of Modernism and the glass sliding wall, and is therefore an invention of the 20th century. However, it is an idea that has been current for centuries, even in the unlikely setting of cold Northern Europe. The Picturesque movement in the early 19th century is perhaps the prime example: in this period plants were used to strengthen the relationship between the interior and its surrounding landscape.

Above A late 18th-century silhouette which shows that the cultivation of house plants was one of the major amusements of genteel society in the period. The simple staging shown here could easily be devised for a present-day collection.

Left A depiction of an Italian study c.1460 shows the importance of plants as decoration, though they might also have been valued as medicinal herbs or as a collection of rarities. They are planted in elaborate majolica pots, possibly to emphasize their significance.

Right An early 19th-century drawing room leads to a conservatory full of plants, some of which have colonized the room itself. Purpose-made plant stands, such as the jardinière (right) were common in the period. The wallpaper with birds and plants continues the idea of the garden brought indoors, one of the main themes of the late Biedermeier interior.

The use of indoor plants and of mirrors positioned so as to reflect the landscape or garden into the room eventually led to the arrival later in the 19th century of a whole style of interior decoration that was inspired by gardens and nature. It was perhaps at its peak in the Biedermeier interiors of Germany, Austria and Scandinavia (see p.8). Many items of furniture were specifically designed for indoor plants in this period. The art of creating tables with zinc-lined recesses, troughs with screens for supporting climbers, and trellises for banking up great mounds of flowers and foliage was perfected at this time.

This period was also the high point of the conservatory. The garden staff of large houses worked closely with members of the household to provide delicate plants, nurtured in the controlled environment of the glasshouse, to decorate the living room for a temporary period. While this explosion of indoor planting was taking place

Above This Copenhagen drawing room of the 1840s uses windowsill plants to good effect. Particularly interesting are the ivy screens in the central window that have gaps to look out through. Such screens provided privacy in towns and are a device that could be adapted for use today.

in grander houses, a similar enthusiasm for plants was taking root in cottages, where the inhabitants continued to grow plants that had been fashionable among the rich in earlier eras. Our image of the old-fashioned country cottage comes largely from the late-19th-century rediscovery of the visual charm of cottage life, and is closely connected with the Arts and Crafts movement. The views of cottage interiors by Helen Allingham in England and Carl Larsson in Sweden (see right) show cottages with both the furniture styles and often the plant fashions of previous times. The same fashion time-lapse occured in other parts of the world. The author Edith Wharton describes grand American drawing rooms of the 1870s as 'full of banked cinerarias and primulas', a combination that fifty years later belonged to much humbler settings, and which would be sneered at by the fashionable in the mid-20th century.

The revolution in architecture and interiors brought about by Modernism has given an enormous potential role to indoor plants. The increased ratio of glass to wall has made interiors lighter and therefore more

Below A Swedish room, illustrated by Carl Larsson, is testament to the late-19th-century Arts and Crafts interest in cottage interiors. This same unselfconscious arrangement of plants on a windowsill is found in country interiors in a wide range of cultures and periods, including Shaker households.

plant-friendly. Tall, bold plants come into their own as 'living screen' room dividers in open-plan spaces and the free, less defined approach to room arrangement has made it possible to devote large areas to planting.

The pages that follow offer a wide range of ideas for the use of plants as an integral part of interior decoration. Many inspired by historical sources, some by the 20th century and some entirely new.

Above A Richard Neutra interior of the 1950s in the Ojai Desert, California. His designs are the ultimate in the fusion of indoors and outdoors, in which the interior planting is devised to blur the distinction between the two. The antithesis of cosy, in this style planting provides the foreground to the landscape beyond and does not so much furnish the room, as extend it into the great outdoors.

RURAL STYLE

Previous page *Chamaelaucium uncinatum* 'Snow Flake' has found a perfect niche in a bathroom with wonderfully distressed, white-painted panelling that echoes the greyish foliage of the plant. It has charming white flowers and forms a compact ball of flowers and foliage.

Right A profusion of narcissi (*Narcissus* 'Paperwhite') massed in a tin footbath draws the eye. The flowers' glorious scent fills the room, offering a foretaste of spring on grey winter days.

Below A pine chiffonier is an elegant frame for begonias. Ochre walls and rust-coloured cache-pots make a perfect foil, bringing the lush colour and velvety texture of the leaves into focus.

The key to rural style is simplicity. Plants should look controlled, like a well-ordered garden, and common cottage plants are definitely the best choice. For an instant and delightful rustic effect nothing is better than such plants as geraniums, primulas or auriculas in plain containers – old terracotta pots, seedboxes, baskets or wooden trugs, which look as if they might have come straight from the potting-shed.

Pictures of rural interiors are a good source of inspiration. The work of Carl Larsson, the 19th-century Swedish Arts and Crafts illustrator and artist, for instance, shows windowsill plant arrangements set off by white walls and plain-white muslin curtains. His plants, which are virtually the only colour in the room, are always in the plainest clay pots, sitting on attractive old saucers or plates. The cottage interiors of the English artist Helen Allingham, of a similar period, may also provide ideas. She takes a rather different view from Larsson, depicting cosy dark interiors with plants in clay pots, standing in old blue-and-white or stoneware kitchen bowls, framed in small, often leaded windows.

Kitchens

The rural kitchen is the hub of family life. It is more than a functional place to prepare food; it is where we gather to eat, talk and socialize, especially in winter when it is often the warmest room in the house. Since so much time is spent in the kitchen it makes sense to pay particular attention to the plants that are housed there.

As well as growing forced flowering bulbs in the living room and other reception rooms, consider putting a few bowls in the kitchen, where they can make the most impact and give the greatest pleasure. The kitchen will be suffused with the scent or colour of flowers for much of the year, from the time when the crocuses of early spring appear to the arrival of cyclamen in late autumn.

Kitchen plants need not be merely decorative: well-kept pots of fragrant herbs look stunning and are wonderfully convenient for cooking and garnishing. A number of plants are suitable for growing in pots on a windowsill. Marjoram, thyme, sage, chives, rosemary, parsley and basil will all do well for a season. If you have space outdoors it is a good idea to rotate your indoor herbs with a similar group of plants outside, so that each group has the benefit of full daylight for part of the year.

Left A zinc splashback adds a modish patina to this country kitchen. Here dwarf white cyclamen have been planted in an old zinc liner and placed on a shady windowsill, where their delicate flowers and marbled foliage are offset most effectively by the sombre colour of the walls.

Left Plants can be effective in all parts of the house, including service areas. In this back hall, bright yellow flowers of narcissus (*Narcissus* 'Tête-à-Tête') have been planted in a plain Victorian basin to add a cheerful burst of colour to the creamware.

Plants need not be relegated to the windowsill in the kitchen. They may be moved, for example to the table when required for mealtime decoration. One idea is to place three or four mop-heads of herbs in identical pots in a line down the middle of a long narrow table. They have the advantage of not obscuring the view across and they look amusing – like miniature versions of the clipped herb bushes seen in Italian Renaissance paintings. Shrubby herbs, such as sage, thyme, rosemary, lavender, bay and myrtle, are suitable subjects. Start by training a main leader to a height of 12–15cm (5–6in) on a short cane, then nip out the leader to start a small mop-head. Keep it compact by nipping out the growing points regularly. Alternatively, a pot of young compact herb, like parsley, marjoram or mint, makes a good centrepiece for a round kitchen table, providing a fresh clean aroma as a bonus, while a saucepan planted with ornamental cabbage on the table (see p.21) provides an element of fun.

For decorative purposes, several pots of the same plant can have more impact than a series of different specimens. On the whole, large groups of the same plant in the same colour work much better than mixed compositions with different colours. They can be massed together in the same holder or spaced out in a row in individual pots, in imitation of a kitchen garden's orderly rows.

Too many different species in close proximity can be visually disastrous. The exception to this, however, is if the desired effect is jungle, in which case the style of decoration in the kitchen should reinforce the conservatory-like appearance provided by the plants. To produce a virtual wall of foliage, try positioning tiers of white-painted slatted shelves (like greenhouse staging) near a window. Choose a selection of plain green foliage plants with different leaf forms, and grow them in shallow zinc or galvanized drip trays the width of the slatted shelves. To achieve a seamless wall of foliage it is effective to mix erect and trailing plants, and to avoid spiky leaves and variegated foliage. In a sunny kitchen you will soon have a lush, living wall of greenery.

Right A row of picturesque and aromatic rosemary shrubs (*Rosmarinus officinalis*) is an inspired way to decorate the table on a hot summer's day. The herb has been trained into small mop-heads, roughly 25cm (10in) tall, and placed in attractive weathered terracotta pots.

Left The Boston fern (*Nephrolepis exaltata* 'Bostoniensis') makes a large and bold enough ball of foliage not to add extra busy detail to a kitchen. Kitchens are often visually complex with a lot of disparate equipment and detail, and to counteract this planting should be large and simple.

Right Simple ideas can work well: the clipped shape of the rosemary shrub complements the white wood and stone flags of this country kitchen perfectly. The pliable stems of three young rosemary plants (*Rosmarinus officinalis*) have been plaited together to create an eye-catching yet simple shape.

As in any room, the choice of plants is determined by what will grow in the prevailing light, temperature and humidity conditions (see pp.112–32 for advice on choosing plants). Rural kitchens can be difficult to furnish with plants, since the kitchen is generally the warmest room in the house. Nevertheless, most have cool spots such as windowsills distant from radiators and cookers. Cool sculleries, larders or utility rooms may be particularly suitable for growing plants – provided that they receive sufficient light.

So many kitchen vessels make ideal jardinières for plants that there is no need to invest in special containers. Many households already have cream-coloured dairy bowls, ceramic jars for dry foodstuffs, 'earthenware' crocks, metal buckets or wooden tubs, all of which conjure up an immediate air of rusticity, especially when planted with herbs. Be inventive when thinking about containers: discarded bread tins, culinary moulds – even a galvanized baby-bath – can all be put to good use. Plain clay pots (preferably old and hand-thrown) with glazed waterproof saucers are also ideal. Old aluminium or enamel trays and pretty pottery plates and saucers are excellent for standing plants on. However, bear in mind that the general style should be simple. Plants can also be grown in black plastic pots (black is less obtrusive than other colours) which are then placed in other, more attractive, containers. If plants are housed in a drainless container or jardinière the roots are susceptible to unnoticed waterlogging, so it is important to be vigilant and monitor them with care.

Left These four dumb cane plants (*Dieffenbachia compacta*) like to bask in warmth and humidity. Their large, strongly shaped variegated foliage works well in a very simple black and white kitchen.

Right Gorgeous ornamental cabbage (*Brassica oleracea*) adds amusement to the kitchen table. Its beautiful purple and grey colours go well with the silver of the aluminium saucepan. Other vegetables such as carrots, tomatoes and aubergines also make fun ornamental plants.

Left A shallow trough planted with culinary herbs against floor-to-ceiling windows creates a visual link with the garden and the plants beyond. The aromatic herbs include golden marjoram (*Origanum vulgare* 'Aureum'), two sorts of golden thyme (*Thymus serpyllum* and *T. vulgaris* 'Aureus'), spearmint and basil mint.

Living Rooms

As well as adding personality and colour, plants also contribute greatly to a country sitting room's rural style. Help the room reflect nature with a changing display of seasonal planting – using different plants you can change the mood to suit autumn, winter, spring or summer. Alternatively, you can furnish the sitting room with plants that compensate for what is lacking in the garden at any particular time. In winter, for example, filling the room with warm-coloured scented plants and bowls of forced spring bulbs gives a welcome foretaste of longer, sunnier days. Later on, in spring, decking the room with early flowering geraniums, scented jasmine (*Jasminum polyanthum*) or the various citruses creates the illusion that summer has come early.

In country sitting rooms a few large plants are more effective than a mass of small ones. Flanking fireplaces or windowsills with pairs of mature plants in matching simple containers gives an elegant effect. Alternatively, plants may be placed on identical side tables. In summer, foliage plants such as the Queensland umbrella tree (*Schefflera actinophylla*), which tolerate shade well, may be placed in front of or actually in the fireplace as a focal point.

Right A large enamel basin easily disguises plastic pots containing Boston fern (*Nephrolepis exaltata* 'Bostoniensis'). The fern's mass of bright green foliage in the centre of this simply furnished room catches the eye, drawing attention to the elegant swan and to the stunning view of the moat and woodland beyond.

Right The short-lived tulip season is one of life's pleasures. The subtle dark purple of these 'black' tulips blends beautifully with this corner of a rural sitting room and contrasts well with the brightly coloured spring cut flowers. It is a shorter variety of tulip, suitable for pot cultivation as it does not need support.

Small plants in the sitting room are better grouped together rather than spread at random, and one way of doing this is to mass them on metal or wood staging in a window.

Look for large containers that will act as interesting informal jardinières. Objects not originally intended for plants, but which work well, include shallow dairy or laundry tubs, seedboxes and old knife-trays for a mass of small plants, and grain measures, butter tubs, buckets and baskets for large single specimens. (Remember that wooden and basket-work containers need saucers or waterproof liners.)

The sitting room is often a difficult environment for house plants since the temperature fluctuates, particularly in winter when the room is heated for use in the evening. The summer suits the plants better as the temperatures is stable. The dry winter atmosphere of many sitting rooms also means that some foliage plants need frequent misting. When considering plants for permanent residence in a sitting room, make sure they can tolerate a dry atmosphere and extremes of heat.

Above The foliage of this cinnamon-scented pelargonium perfumes the sitting room whenever it is brushed against. This plant looks particularly at home in its rural, old-fashioned surroundings, complementing the brown tones of the furniture and straw work.

Right The unaffected native primrose (*Primula vulgaris*) is a perfect decoration for this minimalist 19th-century Shaker parlour in The American Museum in Britain, Bath. Its muted pale yellow flowers add to the feeling of spring tranquillity.

Far right A painted, coopered tub on a low stand in a mid-18th-century parlour at The American Museum in Britain, Bath, shows how visually effective unusual containers can be. It holds laced primulas, whose bicoloured flowers are particularly suitable for their historical surroundings since they were greatly prized in the 18th century.

Left A flowering floor-standing pot of *Nerine* spp. adds a lovely patch of colour to the cool tones of this library and contrasts well with the vertical geometry of the books and bookcases.

Right The jade plant (*Crassula ovata*) has a satisfactory tree-like shape which is well framed by the study window. Its desert origins help it tolerate day-to-night temperature differences, making it suitable for a room that is occupied only by day.

Below Delicate-looking early snowdrops (*Galanthus nivalis*) rising out of moss lift the spirits of tired deskbound workers in mid-winter. Bulbs planted in shallow clay pots in early autumn may be brought into the house to flower before those in the garden.

Studies

Species with small, jewel-like flowers are ideal on a desk or bureau, as they reward close inspection. Snowdrops, lily-of-the-valley, jasmine or myrtle are good choices – and the last three have the bonus of being strongly scented. In the larger context of an office, a study or a library, tough serviceable plants, which will survive erratic care if not actual neglect, are usually needed. Many of the succulents are suitable, for example the jade plant (*Crassula ovata*), century plant (*Agave americana*) and the strikingly marked partridge-breasted aloe *(Aloe variegata)*, the last two of which were introduced into Europe in the 16th and 17th centuries from North America and Africa. Placed on top of bookshelves they catch the eye, giving a small library or study the appearance of a 'cabinet of curiosities'.

Halls and Corridors

Often it is possible to tell the occupant's attitude by the plants kept in halls and corridors. A true plant-lover does not decorate the living room with exotics and leave the landing occupied with just an ailing spider plant! Furnishing these spaces with plants pays enormous dividends, helping to pull the overall rural style of the home together. What's more, plants come into their own in halls, lobbies, landings and corridors, where there may be little room for furniture but generally enough floor or windowsill space for pots. In addition, the circulation spaces of houses tend to be cooler than living spaces, which suits the many species that hate over-heated rooms. A disadvantage of halls and corridors, of course, is that they tend to be dark, but with a little care and careful choice of plant species this is not an insurmountable problem.

Plants that add a rustic touch to the hall and are easy to grow include ivy, aspidistra, box, *Cyperus* and *Fatsia*. Ivy and box in particular create an indoor/outdoor air to an entrance and, if they are trained or topiaried, bring the structure and feel of a formal garden inside. The sides of a narrow hall, for example, could be lined with topiaried box in troughs.

Far left The luxuriant umbrella grass (*Cyperus alternifolius*) has found an ideal niche in this cool corridor next to a window, but it will have to be moved if the temperature drops below 10°C (50°F) in winter. Its clay pot disguises a plastic one, which is needed to help the plant retain moisture.

Left Ivy (*Hedera helix*) looks well against dark colour schemes. The plant is useful for indoor topiary and for training over wirework or chicken-wire forms, and can tolerate low light levels. Here, in the late-17th-century staircase hall at The American Museum in Britain, Bath, ivy grows over a ball made of two wire hoops.

Below False aralia (*Schefflera elegantissima*) can grow to 2m (6ft), but when young it makes an ideal house plant. Its beautiful, almost black, foliage is silhouetted against the light coming in from the window in this upstairs corridor. A 19th-century tin wine-bottle carrier is used as a cache-pot.

These can be punctuated with balls or pyramids to look like an escape from a parterre. Alternatively, box can be raised to head height for a striking hall decoration (see opposite). Such a stand would also suit a less formal cascade of green ivy. Tall thin plant-stands are particularly useful in narrow spaces where there is no room for more substantial furniture, and there are numerous period plant-stands available. Alternatively, a simple wood plinth about 23cm (9in) square and 1.2m (4ft) high is easy to make, or you can improvise with items such as metal saucepan racks or wirework vegetable racks.

It is not difficult to see why aspidistras were once the most popular of house plants; they are extremely attractive and will survive low light levels and the rigours of a hall climate. Though native to China and Japan, they remind me of Italy where they are deployed everywhere as terrace pot plants. Their only disadvantage is the slowness of their growth. They look best in large clumps, and big specimens are expensive, but if you are prepared to buy a plant with only a few leaves and patiently wait for it to grow, aspidistras make very good-value hall plants.

Below Simple topiarized shapes go well with the minimalist detailing of this cottage entrance hall. The double-ball box topiary in the background 'reads' well against the white-painted brick and contrasts with the bushy golden euonymous (*Euonymous fortunei* 'Emerald'n'Gold'). Together they create an indoor/ outdoor feel which suits this rural hall.

Left Entry halls cry out for dramatic plant decoration such as this. Artificial box has been twined round a metal column filled with moss. A topiarized ball of real box (*Buxus sempervirens*) sits at the top. A cool country hallway is ideal for box, which is tolerant of draughts. However, it does need light, and will benefit from a summer holiday outdoors.

Aspidistras need to be periodically divided when they get too large for their containers, producing valuable smaller plants for repotting. They may be displayed in polychrome ceramic jardinières on matching stands – a standard 19th-century arrangement – but their fine foliage is also well set off in plain terracotta pots or the ridged and festooned Italian lemon-tree pots.

Bowls of spring bulbs always look welcoming in a country entrance hall, and the cooler atmosphere there makes them last. They remind me somehow of the 1920s, when indoor bulbs were at the peak of their popularity. A long thin basket, windowbox shaped, standing on the floor and filled with daffodils or hyacinths, all of the same colour and variety, is a feast for the senses and has the effect of bringing the garden indoors. A similarly delightful effect can be achieved in summer with troughs of white lilies; Easter lily (*Lilium longiflorum*) or regal lily (*L. regale*) are both suitable.

Above A peace lily (*Spathiphyllum wallisii*) enlivens this inner lobby, its rich foliage echoing the William Morris wallpaper. It is protected from cold draughts, and damp moss within the openwork metal basket helps to keep the humidity high.

Left Croton (*Codiaeum variegatum*), which are available in a wide range of rich leaf colours, have an air of 19th-century opulence. They work particularly well with rich, dark colour schemes, as in this inner staircase hall with its big scale pictures and furniture.

Right French iron plant-staging is an invaluable prop for creating interesting shapes with plants in front of windows. Here, on a staircase landing, the owner has recreated a description by the author Edith Wharton of an arrangement of cineraria and primula in an 1870s American drawing room, using modern hybrids that have the same rather lurid colours favoured in that period.

Bedrooms

A country bedroom should be a retreat – an orderly, restful idyll simply decorated with only a few essential objects and pictures. Plants can add to this atmosphere, and in guest bedrooms can substitute for cut flowers, giving the room an appearance of being lived in and looked after.

It is best to leave dramatic large-scale arrangements or heady fragranced lilies downstairs, and instead opt in the bedroom for plants with subtly scented and coloured foliage, such as the scented-leaved pelargoniums. There were well over a hundred varieties of these, with wonderfully romantic-sounding names like 'Lady Plymouth', 'Attar of Roses', 'Clorinda' and 'Fair Ellen'. Choose a few with interesting leaf colours that blend with the room's colour scheme – there are a myriad of combinations of colours, from lime green to gold and dull red. Pelargoniums have the additional advantage of needing little care.

The muted tones of sweet-smelling herbs also make a soothing background in a bedroom. In his *Family Herball* (1756), Thomas Hills states that an infusion of thyme leaves cures nightmares – and it might be a good idea to have a pot of thyme near the bed to induce restful sleep. Lavender, also, is a particularly useful herb to have in the bedroom. A traditional remedy for sleeplessness, it was an ancient 'strewing herb' used to make rooms smell sweetly, and it even has moth-repellent properties, which can be effective if it is placed near a wardrobe. Other good herbs to have in the bedroom include rosemary, sweet marjoram and sage, which will all grow well on a windowsill. Herbs can look particularly appealing if they are topiarized into small balls, short standards or low, even mounds. Old illustrations often show indoor plants trained in this way, sometimes in handsome *majolica*, brass or bronze urn-shaped pots – the sort of container that would particularly suit a book-filled oak-panelled bedroom.

If you are not in the bedroom much during the day, or are away during the week, it is easy to overlook the resident plants, so either choose species that can withstand neglect or think in terms of keeping plants in pots in the garden and bringing them inside at the weekend. Good plants for this include standard lavenders, primrose (*Primula vulgaris*) and the primula *P. acaulis*.

Left This charming pair of lavender plants, trained as miniature standards, demonstrates the effect of plants in pairs as part of a shapely symmetrical arrangement. These two are exactly the right size to stand sentry on this painted Pennsylvanian Dutch chest of drawers in The American Museum, in Britain, Bath.

Right *Primula obconica* is a large-flowering variety of primula, available in a number of pretty colours. It has a simplicity that goes well with this early 19th-century stencil-panelled bedroom at The American Museum in Britain, Bath, and is a good choice for a coolish bedroom where its flowers will last longer.

Some might like to take their decorative inspiration from the Biedermeier period of the early 19th century when bedrooms and other rooms were literally, in some cases, transformed into gardens. A plethora of specially designed plant furniture was available – table jardinières, stands and troughs with trellis upstands for climbers. Plants were trained to form screens on wirework forms of various shapes. The wreath form was a popular motif, and it is one that is easy to make and looks particularly stylish. A circular frame can be made with a bent piece of wire (a coat hanger is ideal). The two ends are pushed into the pot at its perimeter, and the plant is encouraged to grow round the wire. Plants that are suitable for this treatment include passion flower, jasmine, stephanotis, ivy, plumbago and many other climbing plants. Plastic frames are also available with pre-trained plants, although these are not as attractive as home-made frames. A number of plant supports can be found in different shapes including lyres, scrolls, balls and spirals.

Footbaths, once a ubiquitous bedroom accessory, make particularly well-shaped large containers for bedroom plants, and old examples are still to be found in painted or galvanized tin, ceramic and enamel. Some examples are now expensive, but it is still possible to buy galvanized or enamel ones cheaply. They can be either left alone or painted or grained. Alternatively, modern reproductions are available. They are best used as cache-pots, with the plant or plants staying in their individual pots. A wide range of bedroom accessories from the past also make good containers – basins, pails and chamber pots.

Left Passion flower (*Passiflora caerulea*) is a vigorous climber that looks good tightly trained on a hoop in the form of a wreath – a device that goes well with the French-Empire style of this bedroom. It needs as much sun as it can get, and should be kept moist in summer.

Right The creamy-white variety of poinsettia (*Euphorbia pulcherrima*) is a restful choice for a bedroom and looks especially stylish in an all-white setting. Three plants fill this grained tin footbath to give an abundance of foliage. Poinsettias stay in flower (the 'flowers' are in fact coloured bracts) for months, so they are good plants to use when planning a bedroom's décor.

Bathrooms

Now that most bathrooms are well heated, even in the country, there is plenty of scope for furnishing them with plants. Moisture-loving ferns like delta maidenhair (*Adiantum raddianum*) thrive in them. For a more exotic touch, try growing bananas (*Musa paradisiaca*, *M. velutina* or *M. acuminata* 'Dwarf Cavendish'); they need humid conditions and often thrive in a warm bathroom. Baby's tears (*Soleirolia soleirolii*) also does well. It looks particularly good growing in large shallow pots to make green cushions (unfortunately not to be sat on).

For long soaks in the bath, looking out at a picturesque rural scene, wonderfully fragranced plants such as hyacinth, tuberose (*Polianthes tuberosa*) and lily-of-the-valley (*Convallaria majalis*) add to the atmosphere, making a bathroom in the country feel luxurious and sybaritic.

Cool bathrooms in old cottages, which perhaps are only used at weekends, need altogether tougher plants, like ivy, crassula or aspidistra that can withstand cold and little watering. On the whole I cannot say that I like variegated forms of ivy, but there are a number that have interesting leaf shapes and sizes – *Hedera helix* 'Colymii' (triangular leaves), *H. sagittaefolia* (long thin points) and *H. canariensis* (large plain green leaves) – which would look interesting trailing from a shelf or trained on a wire frame.

Left Dutch white hyacinths (*Hyacinthus orientalis* 'L'Innocence') enliven this simple grey and white bathroom. Their smell, which evokes expensive floral soaps is perfect for the bathroom.

Far left Ivy (*Hedera helix*) is allowed to trail attractively without the guiding hand of art along the width of the bathroom windowsill. Ivy was one of the most popular plants of the 19th century, and since the 1950s it has once again become valued for its versatility as a plant that can be used either formally or with picturesque irregularity.

FORMAL ELEGANCE

ormality of arrangement is applicable to a wide range of dates and styles. A classical 18th-century drawing room, of course, is a prime example, but certain types of modern interior can be very formal – the 'contemporary meets classical' look of Fleur Rossdale's London home (see p.53), for instance. In most houses the best room, where the owners entertain, often has a strong formal style.

Rooms stuffed with a wide variety of plants tend to be too visually complex for an ordered effect. The key to successful formality is to organize furnishings carefully, maybe in symmetrical groupings. On the whole, less is more: it is preferable to have just a few species of well-chosen plants. However, pairs or groups of four or more plants are useful – possibly two large and two small specimens of the same plant. It is important to consider parts of the room that would benefit visually from the animating effect of foliage and flowers and then to try to match the prevailing conditions carefully to the plant. Think about whether a plant should be large and floor-standing, or if a smaller plant placed on a piece of furniture would look better. Bear in mind where people first see the plant: the traditional site – the windowsill – is seldom a good position for plants in a formal room from a visual point of view.

Previous page A tall green tin florist's vase gives winter jasmine (*Jasminum polyanthum*) height. Vertical proportions suit dining table plants as they help to diversify a table-scape. As it is a vigorous climber it needs rigorous pruning to keep its shape.

Left The grey-tinged foliage of a New Zealand tea tree (*Leptospermum scoparium*) has been trained and clipped into a standard or ball to bring formal gardening indoors. Its vertical line goes well with the strong verticals and horizontals in the furniture.

Right A pair of small winter cherries (*Solanum capsicastrum*) in clay pots painted white look like miniature oranges and add a festive Christmas air to the mantelpiece. Their round fruit echoes the glass lustres on the candlestick.

Kitchens

A formal kitchen will be more organized than most and may be a multi-purpose room, part kitchen and part semi-formal dining room. It is useful to have plants that will fulfil two functions, both to provide everyday decoration, and to act as a focal point when the room is being used for a supper party. For special occasions plants could be re-arranged on working surfaces where they might ordinarily be in the way (see *Agave* below).

Where a kitchen has a particular colour scheme, it is effective to match foliage as well as flowers to it. Variegated foliage can be a welcome relief from green indoors and, provided that its colour combinations are controlled, can work well. Plants with attractively muted variegation include pelargoniums, euonymous, ivy, aspidistras, and grasses such as varieties of *Carex* and *Chlorofitum*. Plants with silver foliage look spectacular in kitchens that have predominantly neutral or metallic materials. Subjects that fit the bill include *Agave* varieties and succulents such as *Aloe* and *Echeveria*, as well as eucalyptus. Suitable containers in such a setting include plain terracotta pots, white-glazed cache-pots and urns. Silver finishes such as galvanized or cast iron, aluminium or lead go well with a kitchen setting.

Left Century plant (*Agave americana*) is a subtle blue-grey colour – the colour of well-patinated copper – and its large leaves make a strong sculptural statement in this blue-grey kitchen. It needs to be carefully sited so that its sharp spikes stay out of the cook's way.

Right Pale variegated foliage of scented geranium and a small mop-head of Japanese spindle (*Euonymous japonica*) make a restful and sophisticated table-scape that goes well with the pale grey and cream of this kitchen.

Humble spider plants (*Chlorophytum comosum* 'Vittatum') come into their own. They have been used to great effect by being placed in grand cast-iron urns. Standing sentinel flanking the door they contribute to the indoor/outdoor effect, leading the eye out from the kitchen into the conservatory.

Living Rooms

Formal sitting rooms are where symmetry and grandeur are appropriate, and where large-scale planting, or groups of small plants, will work well.

As a general aid to thinking about which plants will be successful, begin by considering parts of the room that will benefit visually from the animating effect of foliage and flowers, and then try to match the prevailing conditions to the plant. Consider whether the planting should be large and floor-standing, or smaller to stand on furniture. The traditional place for a plant, the windowsill, is not the ideal place from a visual perspective in a formal room, though proximity to a window is obviously necessary. Two of the same plant on a side table or pier table between windows look well, as do pairs generally in formal settings. As in a garden, one could consider structuring the planting into two categories – permanent and seasonal. A permanent framework of plants with year-round effect may consist of plants such as house lime (*Sparrmannia africana*) or ivy (*Hedera helix*). This could be supplemented by a changing display of seasonal flowering plants.

As well as using plants to make a lively room for everyday purposes it is possible to create dramatic displays for entertaining. In the past, owners of large houses would have had lavish banks of plants – palms and flowers – brought indoors for parties from well stocked glasshouses.

Above *Dendrobium* 'Emma White', one of the many orchids that can be grown indoors given the right conditions, is shown here against a Japanese screen in a Chinese bowl. Orchids are exotic and slightly decadent looking, and their heady scent reinforces this feeling of hot-house excess.

Left Kentia palm (*Howea forsteriana*) planted in a large Chinese blue and white jardinière together with an 1880s Aesthetic Movement chair give this sitting room a very convincing period feel. It was the taste for Middle Eastern exoticism (even though the *Howea* comes from Oceania) that made palms such popular plants in 'artistic' houses.

Right Large plants in very high-ceilinged or double-height rooms make them seem less intimidating without diminishing their grandeur. The Kentia palm (*Howea forsteriana*) shown here has been used both downstairs and on the gallery, giving a unity to the rather different decorative schemes of the two spaces.

This is not an option for most people, but keeping plants in moveable containers in the sitting room is a good idea, so that they can be placed outside for respite when not required; the portable parterre of box (see p.51) comes into this category. Containers of evergreen plants can be arranged in a variety of configurations – under low windows, for example, or organized to flank a door or line a hall for a party.

Plants massed together look dramatic; even the most boring evergreen can look spectacular in a large indoor bank. You need several large plants of a single species to do this effectively, and trees or shrubs with dense habits look best. Try the once despised *Aucuba japonica* (plain or spotted), myrtle and camellia species out of flower, or trees that will tolerate indoor conditions such as silk bark oak (*Grevillea robusta*) and blue gum (*Eucalyptus gunnii*). Clip or pinch the ends of these to keep them compact. Either range plants of different height or use staging or tiers in 30cm (1ft) increments. Cut flowers of a single species arranged, or rather not arranged, as large tight bunches give a satisfyingly simple effect. Several house plants can be relied on to produce the same look, which works particularly well in formal settings and especially in sitting rooms. The most common is pot chrysanthemum (*Chrysanthemum morifolium*); the variety 'Charm' is the most

Above Simple arrangements often have the greatest impact in formal settings, as the daisy-like flowers and grey foliage of floss flower (*Argyranthemum frutescens*) show. Six plants have been massed in a giant terracotta urn to create a gloriously abundant display that is over 1m (3ft) in diameter.

Right In this corner, set up for an intimate conversation, an indoor box 'hedge' (*Buxus sempervirens*) has been created interspersed with small mop-head standards that form a miniature parterre. The hedge echoes the foliage outside and gives a foreground frame to the garden beyond.

Far left A vast kangaroo vine (*Cissus antarctica*) adds an ivy-clad-ruin effect to this imposing living room. It is perfectly placed to receive plenty of light from the window and relates well to the height and proportions of the room. A plant like this is a good substitute for a blind or muslin curtains, shielding the occupants from the eyes of passers-by.

Left The flowers of New Zealand tea tree (*Leptospermum scoparium*) tone beautifully with the opulent Chinese wallpaper and rich red velvet chair in this modern drawing room inspired by the 18th century. Despite its exotic looks, New Zealand tea tree survives well in the house or in a cool conservatory. It should spend some of the summer outdoors.

Below Four pots of Texan bluebell (*Eustoma grandiflorum*) make a restful, classical display in a circular bowl. This corner, in the drawing room of interior design guru Fleur Rossdale, is a good example of her 'Contemporary meets Classical' philosophy in which 18th-century-inspired objects are juxtaposed with modern materials, here represented by the galvanized metal bowl.

densely flowered, forming a solid, wonderfully opulent ball of flowers. Floss flower (*Argyranthemum frutescens*) also produces a dense mass of flowers, as do cineraria, Texan bluebell (*Eustoma grandiflorum*), bellflowers (*Campanula*), busy lizzies (*Impatiens*) and *Hydrangea macrophylla*. If suitably pruned, some shrubs can also have the same look. When clipped, New Zealand tea tree (*Leptospermum scoparium*), for example, produces a solid mass of pale pink or red flowers, and myrtle (*Myrtus communis*) as a clipped ball is spectacular in full flower, though sadly these displays are short-lived.

The same compact, almost topiarized shape can be achieved with various foliage plants. Baby's tears (*Soleirolia soleirii*) can be trained into a low mound, for instance. Massing foliage plants in large urns or vases is another effective technique. If several plantlets of common houseleek (*Sempervivum tectorum*) are planted together on domed-up compost they produce a satisfactorily dense low hemisphere shape, and trail attractively out over the edge of the pot if you let them.

Another effect that suits formal sitting rooms – whatever the period – is a living curtain of foliage large enough in size to form a dramatic set piece. Ivy (*Hedera helix*) is wonderfully versatile in this context and it should be used on a bold scale. It can be used to stunning effect as a continuous frieze at ceiling level, hanging from long shallow troughs fixed high up; the ivy should be clipped so that it trails just enough to hide the trough. This is not an idea that everyone will want to copy, not least because of the difficulties involved in watering the plants, but within the right decorative scheme an ivy cornice looks delightful.

Common ivy (*Hedera helix*) has here been
trained on a conical wire framework and sunk
into 32cm (13in) Versailles cases
for a regimented, period look. A floor-length
mirror cunningly seems to double the
numbers and also reflects back the light,
adding to the airy outdoor effect of this
sunny sitting room. Ivy pyramids are easy
and satisfying to make: place three plants
in each 30cm (12in) pot and train the ivy up
wires, periodically tying in and clipping as
necessary. If the room is heated, the leaves
must be misted regularly.

The charm of ivy is that it can be used as a free-form trailer (see p.56) or as a trained specimen on wirework (see p.54). As a climber on a trelliswork support it can form a dense screen, which is suitable as window curtains (see p.53) or as an internal room-divider, for which purpose ivy was much used during both the 1950s and the early 19th-century Biedermeier period.

Filling a fireplace with plants in summer is a traditional way of creating an animated focal point to the room, and as the plants are only there temporarily the distance from bright light should not be a problem. Flowers are often placed on mantelpieces above fireplaces. For a change, pairs or rows of vases, urns and baskets can be filled with flowering plants to give a similar effect. Use classic urn-shaped white or silver containers filled with bellflowers (*Campanula*), cineraria and white African violets (*Saintpaulia*), or try different chrysanthemum varieties for a tight, formal mound of flowers.

Above Bird's nest fern (*Asplenium nidus*) forms a welcome splash of glossy green against the cast-iron grate and fender. It appreciates plenty of misting as well as shade, so to catch the water the owners have lined its container with plastic, which is concealed with Sphagnum moss.

Left When one sees ivy (*Hedera helix*) like this it is easy to see why Victorian writers such as John Ruskin and Shirley Hibberd considered it to be the most picturesque plant of all, both indoors and out. Here, beautifully framed by the window, its free-form trailing quality comes into its own as it winds down from an old patinated garden urn on a wooden pedestal.

Right Ivy (*Hedera helix*) trained into spheres over wirework frames suits the stellar design of the table-tops in this formal dining room, and tones in well with the foliage depicted in the paintings and tapestries.

Right Almost hemispherical mounds of baby's tears (*Soleirolia soleirolii*) look especially good in these containers: painted cast-iron campagna-shaped urns. Symmetrical arrangements such as this are one of the strongest features of formal style.

Left Few plants are as intrinsically elegant as white camellias. The dark green, glossy foliage of *Camellia japonica* 'Hagoromo' makes a handsome display even when the plant is not in flower, but its white flowers against this warm cream backdrop add a luxurious richness to the scheme. Potted in plastic, this camellia has been mossed and placed in a workbasket on a stand – one example of the many objects that can be drawn into service as planters. Given a cool room and bright light it will last well in flower in spring.

Right In this formal corridor, with its repeat *enfilade* of furniture and pictures, simple arrangements of ivy (*Hedera helix*) and white petunias placed at intervals down the wall make the room look more spacious. In a monochrome setting such as this, coloured plants would look inappropriate.

Bedrooms

There are various ways to decorate a formal bedroom, depending on how it is used. Some bedrooms double as sitting rooms, becoming boudoirs in fact, used for reading, writing letters, chatting on the phone – others are strictly utilitarian, reserved just for sleeping and dressing. In addition, some bedrooms are decorated to suit 'morning' people – with bright, light colours to wake up to (see p.62), while others are designed for night and can be lush and opulent (see right). There are plants to suit all scenarios.

A bedroom designed for reading and contemplation in the morning needs a soothing green plant with not too much scent. A plant with an open, tree-like habit, which can filter early-morning light through its leaves, is perfect. It should be tall enough for it to be possible for the owner to lie in bed and see the morning light making patterns on the wall as it streams in through the leaves. The pale green foliage of house lime (*Sparrmannia africana*) makes a lovely green screen, and spotted flowering maple (*Abutilon striatum* 'Thompsonii') is also suitable, provided that it has an east-facing window and the room does not get too hot. Like house lime it quickly reaches 2.4m (5ft) and will provide plenty of dappled shade.

For a soothing, formal, outdoor-garden look to the bedroom, pairs or symmetrical groups of topiarized Monterey cypress (*Cupressus macrocarpa*) are a good choice. This plant looks hideous outdoors, but surprisingly makes a good indoor topiary subject. The variety 'Goldcrest', which, as its name suggests, is a bright gold-green, is one of the nastiest garden plants, but it looks rather good in a room of an appropriate colour – dark green or white, for instance. It even looks pleasing against bright blue or bright green. Train the plants as clipped standards, pyramids or cylinders and balls and keep them away from direct sunlight. At 2–3m (4–6ft) high they can be floor-standing, and suit plain terracotta pots or plain white tin-glazed containers.

The arum lily (*Zantedeschia aethiopica*), here shown in a 'head' vase by the sculptress Oriel Harwood, completes the look of opulence in this ultimate 'after-dark' colour scheme. The lily was one of the most fashionable flowers of the 1930s – perhaps because it resembles the effect of the bias-cut dresses so popular in that period.

Left An early bowl of primroses brings a foretaste of spring. Common primrose (*Primula acaulis*), seen here, is similar to wild primrose (*P. vulgaris*) but has larger flowers. It makes a good house plant, and its simplicity suits the formal style.

Left Bold scale characterizes this serene monochrome bedroom, and the weeping fig (*Ficus benjamina*) is correspondingly large and simple. Raising the pot just a few centimetres to make the foliage reach the ceiling increases its grandeur and relates the plant to the pictures, which are hung especially high.

When one is designing a bedroom principally for its night-time effect, lighting is an important factor. It is essential to consider how foliage will look under artificial light. Daylight is obviously the most usual form of lighting for plants (and incidentally all plants need a good dose of daylight, to benefit from its UV rays), but it is interesting to see how plants' appearance after dark can be enhanced with clever lighting.

All the best lighting ideas were thought up in the 1930s, and modern lighting technology is only just catching up with concepts formulated over sixty years ago. Tungsten bulbs placed below a ground-glass surface were used in the 1930s to uplight plants and cut flowers, with light fittings designed for that purpose. Today different fittings are available to achieve the same effect. Small, spiked low-voltage halogen spots with low-wattage bulbs – perhaps only 25 watts – are specially designed to be stuck into the soil in a plant pot. They are sufficient to highlight a plant without raising the ambient light levels, which is an important consideration in a bedroom where harsh bright lighting overhead would give quite the wrong atmosphere. Such halogen spots are ideal for uplighting a plant with an open habit and a clear stem of at least 15–30cm (6–12in). Palms, *Dracena* and *Cordyline* shrubs, or large-leaved evergreen foliage plants such as *Fatsia*, *Monstera* or *Ficus*, can all look fantastic lit in this way. To light very large plants you may need to use more than one spot.

Bathrooms

Some might think that a formal bathroom should be a clinical white space, with minimal décor and certainly no plants. However, this is not the case. Plants can contribute greatly to an overall decorative scheme, helping to soften the harsh effect of tiles and enamel which are of necessity usually in evidence.

The bathroom's special environment – warmth, moisture and lack of draughts – makes it possible to grow a range of plants that would struggle in other parts of the house. In a formal bathroom the jungle look with trailing plants is perhaps not appropriate, so instead choose small, exquisite plants that reward close inspection. *Begonia rex* species and angels' wings (*Caladium* x *hortulanum*) both like a moist warm atmosphere and are available in a wide variety of leaf colours and shapes. As always, pairs of plants or carefully chosen groups have a symmetry that particularly suits the formal style.

Both angels' wings and *Begonia rex* can look lurid and definitely showy, which might make them seem a strange choice for a formal bathroom. However, they are certainly not without charm, and they have the distinct advantage of being available in such a wide variety of colour combinations that a plant can be found to match or complement almost any scheme.

Above The quirky, strikingly veined and coloured foliage of angels' wings (*Caladium* x *hortulanum*) suits this Neo-classical bathroom in black and terracotta with Biedermeier furnishings. It is particularly appropriate in this setting since this was the period when plants took over most rooms in the house. Angels' wings thrive in warmth and humidity, so will generally suit a bathroom.

Right The luscious green bank of maidenhair fern (*Adiantum raddianum*) fits in well with the 1930s look of this bathroom. The ferns need shade and humidity and will thrive here above the bath, where they have been placed in blue-and-white cache-pots.

Left The frilly foliage of harts tongue fern (*Asplenium scolopendrium*) softens the severe functionalism of this no-nonsense chrome-and-marble bathroom.

The tiger-spotted *Begonia* hybrid (see above) has a modern look, compared with the velvety, heart-shaped-leaved varieties, and is perhaps particularly suitable for a formal-style bathroom. However, other begonia varieties come in combinations of green, lime, red, cream and brown, which in a richly coloured bathroom add opulence and texture to the walls and tiles.

Ferns are a good choice for a bathroom that has an east or north-facing aspect and may be rather dark. The great advantage of ferns is the fresh bright green colour of their foliage, which both lightens a sombre colour scheme and enlivens a dead white room. They look good in large groups when, massed together, they can make a truly spectacular display. Used in this way, the larger varieties of fern are big enough to make an impact as a floor arrangement.

The maidenhair fern (*Adiantum raddianum*) is a delightfully feathery, light-coloured plant, but for a more architectural look try sword fern (*Nephrolepis exaltata*), which has stiff upward-pointing fronds, or its drooping relation the Boston fern (*N. e.* 'Bostoniensis'). Maidenhair fern really needs to be grouped to make an impact but Boston fern, if placed on a side table or bathroom cabinet, can have a stunning presence on its own or as a pair.

Left The cool metallic colour scheme of this bathroom is set off by a pair of the tiger-spotted variety of begonia, which has been placed in pots that tone perfectly with the walls. Most of this species have a lush 19th-century look, but the tiger-spotted begonia's regular spots give it a markedly contemporary feel.

Below Pristine white *Hydrangea macrophylla* in a simple white cache-pot gives an impression of order and cleanliness in this stylish seaside bathroom. Placing it near the mirror maximizes its impact. Hydrangeas must be kept cool when in flower, during spring and summer, so it would not suit a super-heated bathroom.

COLOUR AND FORM

This chapter explores the striking decorative possibilities of the colours and forms of different plants. Bold effects may be achieved as much from the way that plants are used in the house as from their inherent peculiarities. There are many colourful flowering house plants, but it is what the colour is juxtaposed with, as much as the colour itself, which makes for eye-catching effects. Leaf forms or habits are also included here, though again it is the unexpected juxtaposition that surprises. The term for interesting leaf form, 'architectural foliage', was coined in the 1930s, probably by the Swiss plantsman M. Correvon, and was certainly current by the time Christopher Tunnard published *Gardens in the Modern Landscape* in1938. The term, very pertinent to this chapter, is used to describe plants with bold sculptural foliage that does not necessarily rely on interesting colour or texture for effect, but on shape, outline and the way the plant's overall habit fills space.

Previous page Repeating the simple vertical form of this cactus (*Trichocereus* spp.) gives an architectural clarity to the room, in rather the same way that columns or pilasters divide up a façade. Plants of simple form can often be used to great effect to create this kind of repeat pattern.

Above The striking shade of this sunny yellow wall, the Oriental-looking lacquered table and the caryatid candlesticks by the sculptress Oriel Harwood cry out for a dramatic-looking plant. The strong architectural foliage of Spanish bayonet (*Yucca aloifolia*) fits the bill perfectly.

Left The long narrow leaves of India rubber tree (*Ficus binnendykii*) echo the slats of the Venetian blind satisfyingly. Like all members of the fig family India rubber tree thrives in bright light, which makes this a perfect position for it.

Right A vast spineless yucca (*Yucca elephantipes*) comes into its own in this quirky modern setting. A large plant can be used to provide a visual link with other smaller objects in the room.

Kitchens

Brightly coloured planting can be used in steel and glass kitchens, and also those with primary colour decoration. A large clump of bold-looking plants such as umbrella grass (*Cyperus alternifolius*) or the sedge *C. diffusus* is able to hold its own in a daring colour scheme. *C. papyrus* also has an attractive shape but is less easy to grow. In a similar vein, miniature bulrush (*Scirpus cernuus*) is effective, especially as a repeating pattern of several plants in a row on a windowsill, giving an 'outdoor', grass-like frame to the view. Growing cress in a long shallow trough on a windowsill gives a similar effect. It makes a charming green carpet and, if neatly cropped with scissors, does not look unsightly when partly eaten: rather it has the effect of partly mown grass. Another unusual idea for a kitchen is to grow common or striped pineapple (*Ananas comosus* and *A. c.* var. *variegatus*). They are attractively spiky plants, especially if used in rows as repeat elements (see p.101), and look good with a strong colour scheme. They are surprisingly easy to propagate from a bought pineapple.

Left Long narrow troughs brimming with pansies (*Viola* x *wittrockiana*) have been placed on a slate shelf at eye-level: a fantastically effective yet simple way to add warming colour to a bleak winter room.

Right Explosive-looking umbrella grass (*Cyperus alternifolius*) has been placed against a plain wall, where the shadow of its strongly shaped foliage can make an interesting graphic pattern. Its elegant, rather complex habit goes well with simple modern furniture in Dawna Walter's kitchen (Managing Director of the Holding Company, see p.133 for details).

Living Rooms

Some plants that are not strikingly original can be made so by the context in which they are placed. So, brightly coloured flowers that might look boring in a tastefully muted setting would look spectacular against intense contrasting shades or colour that echoes their own. Hence, orange clivia against lime green has an optical effect, which although not restful is certainly memorable. The intense yellow of sunflower will also look rich and sunny against a deeper shade of yellow. One could have fun divising similar seasonal colour effects, particularly with those flowering house plants bred for lurid colour such as cineraria, chrysanthemum, cyclamen and busy lizzie.

The cactus has undergone a remarkable revival in fashion. To the style-conscious it makes reference to the 1950s and its original discovery as a decorative accessory in what could be described as West Coast Modernist interiors. The all-glass houses by architect Richard Neutra in desert settings with free-form swimming pools are the true home of the cactus – rather a far cry from European '50s magazine *Contemporary* which took the cactus as its favourite house plant, perhaps because of the fashion for Americana and the Wild West.

Of cacti one could probably say the bigger the better. Their sculptural forms work best against plain backgrounds. A collection of small disparate cacti is difficult to make into a satisfactory composition, but large specimens are expensive, so one would have an accruing asset by growing them on in a less conspicuous but sunny part of the house. Consider growing only two or three varieties of contrasting vertical and globular forms. With

Left A bright pink basket used as a cache-pot is a clever choice for this topiarized golden Monterey cypress (*Cupressus macrocarpa* 'Goldcrest'). The colour contrasts with the yellow-green foliage and checked blanket to create a beautifully sunny look in this bright blue-green bedroom.

Right An example of an extremely controlled colour scheme where exactly the right shade of paper flower (*Bougainvillea glabra*) has been found. Bougainvillea has an artificiality of appearance which is good in this context – extremely *de luxe* upholstery in a very simple cottagey building creating a pleasantly surreal environment.

cacti, I tend to think form is all, and that cactus flowers are slightly *de trop*; they often look as if they have landed by accident on the plant. However, many species only flower once a year or, with luck, not at all!

Good, large, vertically formed species are *Trichocereus candicans* (1m (3ft) tall and branching) and *Notocactus leninghausii* (up to 60cm (2ft) tall). The prickly pear (*Opuntia robusta*), a native of the USA but also reminiscent of the Southern Mediterranean, has a good bold form (like stacked rabbits' ears). The latter has lethal spines so one would have to be careful of position. Of globular forms, *Echinocactus grusonii* is good and has the added bonus of seldom flowering.

Much attention needs to be given to the container into which a cactus is planted. Since it needs good drainage it must be a holed one. A cache-pot would need vigilance to make sure that the inner pot was not standing in water. Because form is all with a cactus, try to choose a pot that goes with the shape. Usually a plain colour is preferable so that the texture and subtle colour of cacti can speak for themselves. Hand-thrown terracotta is often a good choice, as is shiny metal in a more Modernist context.

Above The strong sprays of foliage of Kaffir lily (*Clivia miniata*) are elegant even without the flowers. Here its tapered green leaves are set off by the surrounding colours of the chrome, wall and table. The lily is available in orange, red, yellow and cream and makes an exotic display in early spring.

Far left A room where eastern influences meet the classical, combined with modern colour and detailing, means that a fairly bizarre exotic is appropriate. Here, the vertical chunky form of *Cycad encephalatus* admirably suits the large, simply detailed, Indian version of a Regency daybed and is silhouetted against the window to excellent effect. (This picture and the one on the left were taken in Dawna Walters' home, Managing Director of the Holding Company, see p.133 for details.)

Left A fiery orange room conjures up scorching climates, and the prickly pear (*Opuntia robusta*), a familiar sight in the Southern Mediterranean, looks at home and accentuates the desert atmosphere. The tall North African basket serves as a plinth as well as a cache-pot.

Hallways and Corridors

Hallways create the first impression in a house, and colour plays an important role in ensuring an initial welcoming atmosphere, particularly in dark gloomy passageways. Think of flowering plants that have impact and will be immediately memorable, even when one is just passing by. Such seasonal delights as sunflowers, mimosa or *Senecio grandiflorus* provide bold yellow masses that would be highly effective against warm-coloured walls – even paintwork of a different vivid yellow from the flower can be highly successful (see opposite). One could have fun devising a well-planned seasonally changing regime of flowering plants in a narrow colour range, so that, for instance, only orange-yellow or bright cerise was used. With ingenuity a plan could be thought up to accommodate each month of the year.

Space can be at a premium, so think of ways of incorporating plants in a manner that does not encroach on valuable circulation room. Narrow plinths about 1.2m (4ft) high are useful, as are wall-mounted brackets. The latter could be of minimal design – a simple cantilevered-shelf just big enough to hold a cache-pot; or more elaborate – a classical scrolled plaster bracket. Shelves of this sort would be more effective in pairs or groups rather than individually. Small sets of hanging shelves could also be very attractive to show a still-life composition of objects and plants.

Left Cacti need plenty of warmth, especially in winter. This Mexican gem (*Echeveria elegans*) has been planted in a glass jar with layers of moss, compost and drainage gravel, all visible to make decorative strata. Growing a cactus in this way protects it from draughts, shields you from the spines and creates a beneficial microclimate in which the cactus will thrive.

Right Little can beat a sunflower for a cheerful sunny effect. Here a row of dwarf sunflowers (*Helianthus annuus* 'Pacino') bask in the sunny atmosphere provided by the gorgeously rich yellow walls. Although sunflowers were an icon of the Aesthetic Movement they also suit a modern setting such as this. What could have been a sad, overlooked corner of the house has been transformed into a glorious riot of colour.

Bedrooms

Bedrooms are private spaces – the places where people can give free rein to their imaginations and use colour and decoration to create fantasies that might be inappropriate in other rooms of the house. Whether in terms of colour or of scale, bedroom decoration can be as bold or as idiosyncratic as you like. For instant cheer during a dull winter or spring, try importing some of the brightest flowering house plants with vibrant eastern colour. Bougainvillea, which comes in a range of shades from shocking pink to crimson and mauve, will flower from spring to summer. Camellias (in pink, red or white) make the bedroom look luxurious in early spring, and cinerarias, which are also available in a variety of hot colours, help to brighten grey winter light.

Take foreign travel as your inspiration. Southern sunshine can be suggested by the colour scheme of the room, with plants of appropriate colour combinations, such as Aegean bright sea-green, yellow and white, or the startling ones seen in India – emerald green, shocking pink and magenta. The bright yellow-green of certain foliage plants such as Golden Monterey cypress (*Cupressus macrocarpa* 'Goldcrest') and spreading club moss (*Selanginella uncinata*) also help create a very sunny effect.

Other foliage plants conjure up warm climates by association, for example the wonderful spiky agaves and aloes in beautiful grey-greens and variously variegated combinations of green, grey, yellow and white.

Left Paper flower (*Bougainvillea glabra*) has been trained on a hoop and planted in gilded coral planters by the sculptress Oriel Harwood to give the finishing touch to her brightly coloured Indian bedroom. Although bougainvillea needs bright sun, it may be placed in a bedroom temporarily while in flower.

Right *Dracaena compacta* may look topiarized, but this is its natural habit. It retains a dense cluster of foliage, like a small mop-head, a shape that makes it a pleasing bedside-table plant.

Bathrooms

A bathroom does not have to be large to be decorated with startling plant effects. Trailing plants are outstandingly useful here since they make a dramatic curtain of foliage without taking up too much floor space, which is usually at a premium. Trailing plants are usually better in very simple containers since the container is mostly hidden by foliage. An exception would be the sort of quirky 'head' vase seen below.

Placing pots on windowsills may be good for the plants' well-being, but it is seldom visually successful unless they are large, or dramatic, enough to become the focal point of the room. Avoiding a windowsill may not be a problem in good light conditions, but in a dark room go for plants that are tolerant of shade and generally low light levels. Think of placing plants on shelves, lavatory cisterns or bath edges. Trailing plants that tolerate these conditions include heart-leaf philodendron (*Philodendron scandens*) and *Epipremnum*.

Tiny rooms such as bathrooms are the place where little dashes of bright colour from small flowering plants can work. The velvety colour of African violet and busy lizzie for instance, which look insignificant in a large room, can come into their own, especially if seen against dark colours.

Below Devil's ivy (*Epipremnum aureum*) planted in 'head' sculptures by Oriel Harwood, with the tips nipped out to make a bushy hair-like shape. The aerial roots make an interesting contrast with the coral-like hair of the right-hand head.

Left What could be more luxurious than eating strawberries in the bath? The strawberries (*Fragaria* x *ananassa*) are unexpected and amusing indoor plants that demonstrate the way in which strong foliage can have a dramatic effect.

MODERN AND CONTEMPORARY

Previous page From left to right, desert fan palm (*Washingtonia filifera*), sago palm (*Cycas revoluta*) and grass palm (*Dracaena indivisia*) are ideal in this double-height loft space where their spiky foliage and architectural shapes can be seen to great advantage from above.

Left The ubiquitous false castor-oil plant (*Fatsia japonica*) has found its perfect niche in a wide-angled tread of this light, white staircase, where it looks stunning. Many large-leaved foliage plants are best viewed from above, so consider positioning them where they can be seen from staircases or landings.

Right In the foreground the characteristically slashed leaves of a Swiss cheese plant (*Monstera deliciosa*) make an interesting foil for the equally bizarre leaf form of a Kris plant (*Alocasia sanderiana*). The Kris plant's conjunction of leaf and stem gives it the appearance of a Calder mobile, which contributes to the 1950s feel of the room.

The Modern movement in architecture created a new and exciting vision of the potential of indoor plants. Bold foliage effects predominate in contemporary rooms, and large-scale plants come into their own. The austere geometry, simple decoration and light, airy feel that are so often characteristic of modern interiors are ideal foils for large informal displays of massed foliage, in much the same way that the formal and informal are juxtaposed to great effect in gardens – the one giving point and contrast to the other. Simple modern decoration allows plants to play a prominent part in the overall decorative scheme, or even form the dominant element. A single plant with a strong shape, for example, may be used to echo or complement an architectural feature in the room.

Another widespread trend is to blur the division between house and garden with judicious use of indoor plants, so that interiors have a delightful garden-like character. This effect is reinforced by the increasing use of large floor-to-ceiling glass walls which bring the garden, as it were, indoors.

Kitchens

The look of modern kitchens is simple and utilitarian – a style that may be cleverly enhanced with plants, in particular culinary herbs which are as decorative as they are useful. Herbs look best in plain clay pots but may be linked to the overall kitchen décor with appropriate saucers or trays. White-glazed ceramic saucers or shallow galvanized watering trays filled with pea gravel look particularly pleasing in an all-white kitchen, for example. Traditionally shaped white-glazed conical pots also look attractive, as do clear glass pots of the same shape.

Small, tight-clipped bushes of common juniper (*Juniperus communis*) or myrtle (*Myrtus communis*) are an unusual and attractive addition to the more common herbs. Scented-leaved pelargonium has a refreshing aroma; lemon-scented pelargonium (*Pelargonium crispum*) is particularly pleasant to grow in the kitchen. If there is space, a floor-standing bay tree will be appreciated by cooks and also varies the scale of planting. In kitchens with external doors or French windows, a large bay tree can be placed inside or out according to the weather (they need some fresh air to thrive).

Below A collection of culinary herbs (from left to right: rosemary, marjoram, mint, parsley and fennel) furnishes a shelf above the sink, the leaves enlivening the clinical white and chrome of the kitchen. The plants will not last indefinitely but, with care, should provide fresh herbs for a season.

Right The owners of this all-white kitchen have used a standard bay tree (*Laurus nobilis*) to dramatic effect. Its head of aromatic green leaves is at the perfect height for light and for effect. A pot of lily-of-the-valley (*Convallaria majalis*) makes a beautiful scented display in early summer.

Far left The sleek lines of this modern kitchen worktop and its appliances are enhanced by a selection of miniature succulents set in fine gravel in aluminium pots.

Left Heart-leaf philodendron (*Philodendron scandens*) is given a contemporary feel by being set in a pot that matches the Philippe Starck lemon squeezer and the stainless steel sink. It is a fast-growing plant whose glossy foliage may be trained to frame the peep-hole kitchen window.

The kitchen is a multi-functional place at the heart of the home, where we cook, eat and conduct family life. Plants come into their own in the kitchen, softening an otherwise clinical and streamlined environment. However, most people want to avoid cluttering the kitchen which, especially in cities, is often tiny. A good way to add plant interest without taking up a lot of space is to have a collection of miniature plants in very small pots. It is important not to have too many; a few well-chosen specimens are sufficient. The plants must be in matching pots, in immaculate condition and of the same genus, or of similar habits – nothing looks worse than a windowsill or work surface full of ill-assorted or ill-looking plants that have arrived by accident and are there out of pity – one must be ruthless.

Plants situated on a work surface will come under the constant gaze of a busy cook as he or she moves around the kitchen, so it is essential to choose plants that will look good on close inspection. This is where tiny miniature-leaved plants come into their own. Succulents such as varieties of houseleek (*Sempervivum*), string-of-beads (*Senecio rowleyanus*) and ghost plant (*Graptopetalum paraguayense*) fit the bill perfectly.

Controlled climbers look most effective around particular features or used as small screens in the kitchen. Climbers trained on a square galvanized moss-covered frame may be used to emphasize an architectural feature such as a window, a chimney breast or even a wall above a sink. Heart-leaf philodendron (*Philodendron scandens*) is a tough reliable climber for a kitchen and, importantly, will tolerate fairly poor natural light.

Dining rooms

In modern houses dining rooms tend to be multi-purpose, even when they are used primarily for formal dining. House plants can double as table decorations for meals and fulfil a different decorative function – perhaps in a lighter position – for most of the day. Tall thin plants or those with open habits make the best table decorations – large solid clumps of foliage are not practical, nor are spiky or fragile plants. Tall *Cyperus* is a good choice and so is Japanese sedge (*Carex morrowii*) or the grass-like miniature bulrush (*Scirpus cernuus*), which looks especially effective grown through a tube to make a standard. Planting shallow troughs with a carpet of baby's tears (*Soleirolia soleirolii*) or creeping fig (*Ficus pumila* 'Minima') makes an interesting low tablepiece.

Above The shape and height – 45cm (18in) – of these umbrella grasses (*Cyperus alternifolius*) make a dramatic statement on this contemporary dining table. Their vertical see-through habit means that they do not block the view across the table or interfere with conversation.

Right Many species of bamboo thrive as houseplants. Here a halogen downlighter picks out a handsome compact clump of the *extase* variety of bamboo as it bursts from its modern conical glass pot, forming a striking living centrepiece to this dining-room cabinet.

Left The abundant scented yellow flower-heads of *Telanthophora grandifolia* have been used by the owners of the Hotel Tresanton, Cornwall, to dispel winter and create a summery air in the large sitting room.

Right The stems and charmingly untidy tufts of leaves of the multi-stemmed elephant's foot plant (*Beaucarnia recurvata*) create a graphic pattern against the plain wall of this loft sitting room. Ideal for living rooms as it likes a dry centrally-heated environment, it also looks good with the nearby collection of cacti.

Below The impossibly exotic pink flowers of rose grape (*Medinilla magnifica*) are set off to advantage in this simple modern living room. In a less restrained setting they could easily look vulgar, but here they lend the room an immediate air of luxury.

Living rooms

A bold approach is needed in modern living rooms: one large floor-standing plant with an eye-catching architectural shape is worth any number of boring small ones. A big room will, of course, take more than one plant, but it is important to group them in the same style or according to a theme. Perhaps they might all be desert plants, or all have large-toothed or interestingly shaped leaves. The idea of making a 'landscape' of disparate plants, so often attempted in offices and airports, seldom works on a domestic scale – if it ever does, anywhere!

The colour of foliage requires consideration. In a light-coloured room the dark green of unvariegated varieties is invariably most effective. Dark leaves also look good silhouetted against light – in front of large down-to-the-floor windows, for instance, or against an up-lit white wall. Pale or variegated colours look better against darker colours; they need contrast to make the leaf forms 'read', or else they are, in a sense, camouflaged.

A row of weeping figs (*Ficus benjamina*) echoes the plants on the external windowsill. Using plants as a repeat element, in pairs or threes, and planning internal and external planting around a window, gives a substantial and considered effect, which has been used here to enliven the restrained colours and ordered, light feel of this modern apartment. Weeping fig is one of the most useful foliage plants, especially trained as a mop-head standard.

Left Without the magnificent date palm (*Phoenix canariensis*) this minimal interior might appear bland or lifeless. The palm conjures up exotic sunny climes. The pointed and fringed curtain valance reinforces a Middle-Eastern look.

Many modern rooms require the enrichment, in the ornamental sense, of plants to give them interest and to act as a contrast to the simple uncluttered lines of furniture and wall treatment. Plants are, perhaps, the one 'allowable' decoration in the canon of modern design which eschews visual complexity. Bold foliage can add sculptural texture to a room of smooth surfaces. It can also diversify the scale of a room with mainly low furniture, and help break up large plain wall surfaces devoid of pattern or pictures. Consider whether a vertical or a horizontal form is needed. One should also decide what habit of foliage is preferable – the possibilities include a light elegant open leaf formation, a dense solid shape or the controlled forms achievable by topiary or training.

Another consideration is the texture of the leaves themselves as opposed to the overall texture produced by foliage *en masse*. Many plants like the *Gynura* (below) have a velvety texture, and being more reminiscent of fabric than of foliage can add a sense of richness to a room of hard surfaces. These plants are available in rich lurid colours which should be used adventurously rather than worrying too much whether they are in good taste.

Left Here is a prime example of a house plant as a considered accessory. The velvet plant (*Gynura sarmentosa*) is a visual delight: its lush, surreal-looking leaves appear to be made from purple silk velvet. In an amusing gesture the owners have placed it next to a velvet cushion of a similar colour and texture.

Above Bright pink flowers and elegant thin leaves give a tall oleander (*Nerium oleander* 'Rosa Sangue') a sharp modern appearance that accords well with this brightly coloured living room designed by Justin Meath-Baker. In particular, the plant's height suits the vertical emphasis of the room and its furniture.

Above Blackleaved panemiga (*Aeonium arboreum* 'Schwarzkopf') may be a mouthful but it is one of the few near-black plants, making it very useful in monochrome schemes. Here it is a clever addition to the still life in the wacky bar of the Hotel Tresanton, Cornwall.

Above right A pot of purple crocus is reminiscent of Clarice Cliff's Art Deco ceramics – it was one of her favourite motifs. The bright colours of spring bulbs – orange, purple and yellow – suit white modern interiors where strong colours can be introduced, even if temporarily, with impunity.

Right A simple line of striped pineapples (*Ananas bracteatus striatus*) in old clay pots is just the right size to be framed perfectly by the window divisions and the blind above. They give the house a designed, considered appearance when viewed from the outside.

The vast range of colours of different flowers and leaves can be used to enhance décor that has a defined colour scheme. Plants with non-green, monochromatic foliage, for example, can be useful as a quiet foil in some schemes. In the black/ purple range, false aralia (*Schefflera elegantissima*), *Aeonium* and velvet plant (*Gynura*) varieties can all make a real contribution to colour schemes in which green would be out of place.

It is easy to overlook the effect that plants on a living-room windowsill can have when viewed from outside, particularly in town houses where the window and the front garden may be in close juxtaposition. A collection of plants ranged along the windowsill, if it has enough presence, can have just as much impact from the outside as a window box.

From outside, a plant will generally be seen against a dark background since a room, however light inside, always appears dark in contrast with bright outdoor light. For a plant to be seen, therefore, it has to be pale in colour – light variegated pineapple plants are suitable, or perhaps the ubiquitous spider plant (*Chlorophytum comosum*) and the lovely striped *Agaves* and *Aloes*. These also have strong, simple leaf shapes that are easily discernible at a distance. When one is arranging plants it is important to make the planting relate to the shape of the window so that the plants are framed by the glazing pattern.

Halls and Corridors

Above Curly palm (*Howea belmoreana*) is an inspired choice to decorate this dramatic top-lit hall and stairwell. The curves of the fronds follow the lines of the simple staircase balustrade, and the plant is sufficiently large to be clearly visible on both floors.

Stairwells and halls are frequently a dark awkward shape to furnish. Two aspects, however, are in their favour. Firstly, plants may be positioned to be admired from above, which is very often the best viewpoint, especially for those that have large leaves and flat canopies. Plants that look good viewed from a landing to the hall below include species of *Fatsia*, *Monstera*, *Philodendron* and the bigger-leaved varieties of *Ficus*, all of which have bold, interestingly shaped leaves. Secondly, there is the possibility of trailing plants over landings or even down balustrades. This is useful in a small hall, providing an expanse of foliage with minimum loss of floor space. Although trailing foliage might not suit every house it would look good in a light white hall, giving it a conservatory-like appearance.

In a narrow hall it is tempting to place plants near or next to a glazed front door, but this can make the hall look cramped and expose the plant to destructive fluctuations in temperature. A better position, if it suits the layout, is to place plants where they can be seen as people come through the door. Even if this position is darkish, which it often is, some plants such as ivy, aspidistra and heart-leaf philodendron will survive.

Left A ground-floor shot of the staircase illustrates just how big a plant needs to be in a space as grand as this. A collection of small plants would look insignificant by comparison. The curly palm's (*Howea belmoreana*) high canopy means that only the non-usable space of the stairwell void is filled with foliage; the hall itself is unencumbered.

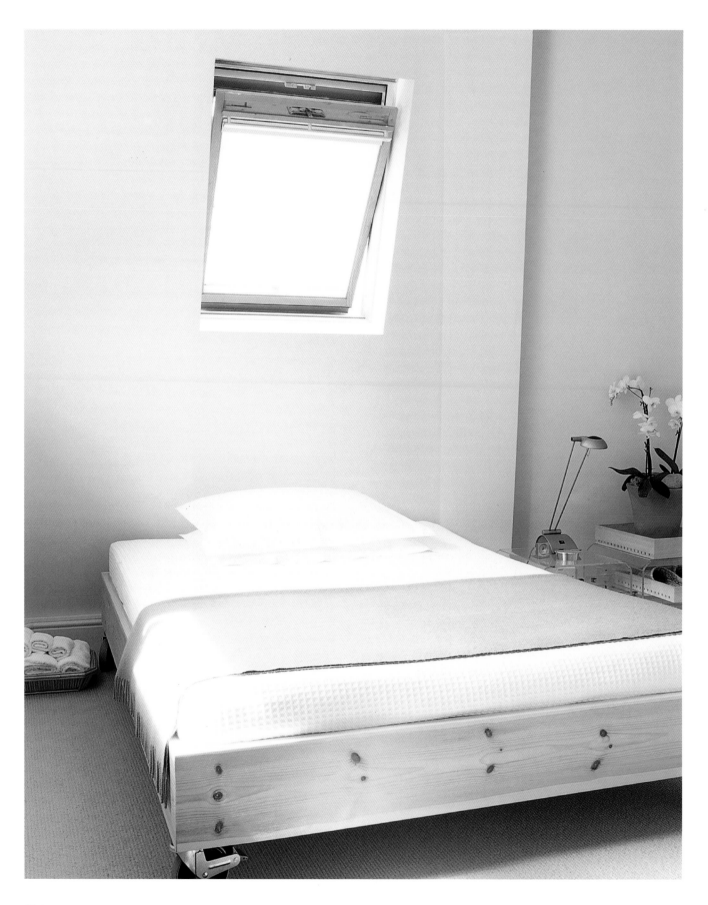

Bedrooms

Cool minimalist bedrooms should not be cluttered with too many plants, but one or two, judiciously placed, can look very effective. Plants in pairs placed on small items of furniture always have a pleasing symmetry. The bedside table is a good place for viewing flowering plants close to – provided that they are not likely to be inadvertently knocked over in the night! Specimens that have interesting leaf forms and habits, as well as flowers, are particularly suitable for a modern bedroom. In this category come the *Cymbidium* orchids with their bold attractive leaf sprays, Japanese pittosporum (*Pittosporum tobira*), which has a dense clump of dark green foliage, and house lime (*Sparrmannia africana*) with its large, pale green leaves and open habit.

It is pleasant to look up into a plant canopy when lying in bed. Plants with spreading umbrella-like canopies, such as palms or the indoor trees *Grevillea*, *Eucalyptus* or weeping fig (*Ficus benjamina*), are all suitable, as long as they are large enough.

Tidiness and order are integral to a minimalist bedroom. Substantial plants can help to divide a bedroom into sleeping and dressing areas, screening clothes, toiletries and other clutter from view. Plants with screening potential include large palms, such as Kentia palm (*Howea forsteriana*), bamboos, ivies and climbing varieties of *Philodendron*. To be used in this way the planting has to be an integral part of the design of the room. It is important to choose troughs carefully, so that they provide solid bases and are of a suitable material to go with the room. Supports for climbing plants like ivy have to blend with both architecture and design, perhaps being made of the same wood that is used elsewhere in the room, or painted to match the walls.

Below The ball-like form of spotted laurel (*Aucuba japonica*) continues the sculptural look provided by the very simple furniture in this geometric, white interior.

Left Waxy orchids have a perfection that suits the minimal décor of this bedroom. This *Phalaenopsis* orchid adds an element of richness that such a restrained interior needs.

Bathrooms

Plants have the effect of softening and humanizing modern bathrooms, which tend to be functional and without superfluous ornament. As with halls, space is often at a premium, so ingenuity is required to find sites in which plants will thrive and not be in the way. Wall-fixed shelves are often the only available space, in which case small, compact plants (*Selaginella* moss, for example) are ideal, or trailing plants such as asparagus fern (*Asparagus densiflorus* Sprengeri Group), baby's tears (*Soleirolia soleirolii*) and mother of thousands (*Saxifraga sarmentosa*). Other good positions include bath edges and windowsills. Where there is space, floor-standing specimens or plants in tall floor-standing containers are perfect as they help to counteract the cubic geometry of a bathroom.

Small-leaved, soft-textured plants are friendly choices for bathrooms – larger, leathery-leaved plants, unless they are well out of reach, both look and feel uncomfortable in this context. Many of the smaller ferns (delta maidenhair or bird's nest fern, for instance) look good as they have bright fresh-green foliage that goes well with the white or neutral colour schemes of many modern bathrooms.

Left Horizontal heads of spider fern (*Pteris multifida*) burgeon out of tall galvanized containers. The soft texture of the fern is an ideal foil for the hard surface of the bathroom, but given the spider-like protuberances at the base of the plant this is not a good choice for the arachnophobe.

Right In this small bathroom, plants are placed on ledges to save on floor space. A living curtain of asparagus fern (*Asparagus densiflorus* Sprengeri Group) cascades onto a pot of baby's tears (*Soleirolia soleirolii*), the different densities of foliage making a pleasing combination.

Right The miniature bulrush (*Scirpus cernuus*) evokes grassy dunes, contributing to the seaside theme of this bathroom. Its pebble-lined glass pot continues this mood, which is set by the collection of seashells in jars.

To avoid the aridity and lack of atmosphere that a modern bathroom can so easily have, it is possible to invent a simple scheme or scenario that adds an element of fun. This need not be fussy, contrived or time-consuming, and is possible to create even in the smallest bathroom. Seaside themes are popular, and are easy to put together with the aid of beach pebbles, shells, simple stencils and a few suitable plants such as grasses or miniature bulrushes (*Scirpus cernuus*). Alternatively, a collection of attractive glass scent, oil, or medicine bottles in different colours could be arranged on a shelf interspersed with glass pots containing scented plants, such as stephanotis or jasmine, with aromatic herbs like myrtle and rosemary. The choice of subject for such schemes is as wide as the range of plants available.

It pays to have clean-looking containers and plants that are kept in the pink of condition, since nothing is more depressing in a bathroom than grubby, ill-looking plants. Galvanized, aluminium, glass or white-glazed pots accord well with a modern bathroom's pristine look. Visible soil seems somehow at odds with the cleanliness of bathrooms, so gravel, pebbles or moss as a top-dressing may be arranged to conceal the compost.

Right Without the miniature pots of bright-green spreading club moss (*Selaginella kraussiana*) the grey, white and silver colour scheme of this seaside bathroom at the Hotel Tresanton, Cornwall, might seem muted or even sombre. The plants bursting out of cache-pots made from aluminium toothmugs add a witty dash of living colour.

PLANT DIRECTORY

bright light, cool

Kangaroo thorn (*Acacia armata*)

In spring the kangaroo thorn produces many small fluffy yellow flowers on stiff branches bearing spine-tipped foliage.

• water freely in spring and summer but very sparingly in winter; feed fortnightly in the growing season

• repot directly after flowering and also prune to shape

• propagate by stem cuttings in early spring

low light, warm

Delta maidenhair fern (*Adiantum raddianum*)

Growing to about 45cm (18in), this fern with its delicate thread-like stems makes a good plant for both pots and hanging baskets.

• water liberally in summer and keep quite moist at all other times; feed fortnightly during the summer

• repot in spring

• propagate by division in spring

bright light, cool

Saucer plant (*Aeonium arboreum*)

Succulent forming rosettes of fleshy foliage with yellowish flowers on a central erect stem.

• keep compost moist in spring and summer and greatly reduce watering in autumn and winter; feed occasionally during full growth

• repot every year in spring, using a free-draining potting compost

• propagate by division of rosettes in spring or leaf cuttings in summer and autumn

bright light, cool

Century plant (*Agave americana*)

A spiny plant with stout, succulent leaves forming a rosette. The various variegated forms are very decorative. When fully grown it can reach over 1.2m (4ft) across.

• water regularly in summer but sparingly in winter; feed every three or four weeks in spring and summer

• repot occasionally in spring

• propagate by offsets when repotting

low light, humid

Elephant-ear plant (*Alocasia* x *amazonica*)

The large arrow-head-shaped emerald-green velvety leaves have a real tropical look. 'Green Velvet' has boldly marked white veins.

• water and feed regularly in spring and summer; keep compost moist in autumn and winter; feed every two months

• repot in spring ensuring good drainage

• propagate by division in spring and summer

bright light, cool

Aloe vera

A succulent with pointed foliage forming rosettes. Yellow tubular flowers are held on a usually unbranched stem up to 80cm (2½ft) high and appear in spring and early summer.

• water and feed regularly during the growing season but greatly reduce in winter; always allow compost to dry out between waterings

• repot or top-dress in late winter

• propagate by cuttings or offshoots in late spring

bright light, warm

Pineapple
(*Ananas comosus* 'Variegatus')

The prickly-edged foliage with its creamy stripe is particularly attractive – white and flushed red. Even the fruit is similarly coloured.

- keep moist at all times
- do not repot; after flowering reduce liquid feeding as suckers are formed
- propagate by suckers removed from roots in spring or root the tuft of foliage on top of fruit

low light, cool
(needs good light in winter)

Norfolk Island pine
(*Araucaria heterophylla*)

A fairly slow-growing evergreen conifer which remains in good condition for several years before losing its lower branches.

- from spring to autumn water freely and feed fortnightly; keep compost just moist in winter
- repot every spring
- propagate by cuttings which can be produced by cutting back old leggy plants to 15cm (6in)

bright light, cool

Marguerite, Floss flower
(*Argyranthemum frutescens*)

A summer-flowering plant with single or double daisy flowers, often with cushion centres. White, pink and yellow forms are available. The divided leaves are held on shrubby stems.

- water freely in spring and summer and keep compost moist in winter; feed regularly
- repot in spring; prune back hard
- propagate by stem cuttings in spring or autumn

low light, cool

Asparagus fern (*Asparagus densiflorus*)

Grown for its clusters of decorative feathery rich-green foliage. There are compact and semi-climbing forms, with the latter reaching a height of 2m (6ft).

- water sparingly in winter but regularly in summer; feed every fortnight
- repot in spring using any good proprietary compost
- propagate by division or seed in spring

low light, cool

Cast-iron plant, Parlour plant
(*Aspidistra elatior*)

A really tough plant from China making few demands; although responding to good treatment it can tolerate a certain amount of neglect, but beware of waterlogging conditions.

- water and feed regularly in summer, and much less frequently in winter
- repot in spring every two to three years
- propagate by division when repotting

low light, humid

Bird's nest fern (*Asplenium nidus*)

The glossy leaves form a rosette from the base, leaving a short sturdy fibrous stem reminiscent of a bird's nest.

- water freely in summer and feed every two weeks; keep compost just moist in spring
- repot in spring
- propagate by offsets which are occasionally formed, and pot these in spring; propagation by spores can be difficult in the home situation

low light, cool

Harts tongue fern (*Asplenium scolopendrium*)

A quite hardy fern with long strap-shaped leaves. There are numerous attractive forms with pleated leaves often with many finely folded edges.

• water and feed regularly in spring and summer; keep compost moist in winter
• repot in spring using an organic-based compost
• propagate by detaching side crowns in spring

low light, draughty

Spotted laurel (*Aucuba japonica*)

The heavily yellow-spotted forms of this glossy foliaged plant are the most attractive. It is tolerant of deep shade and draughty positions, and is happy in cold but frost-free situations.

• water and feed at all times, particularly in spring and summer
• repot and lightly prune, taking care not to cut across the leaves
• propagate by cuttings in spring and autumn

bright light, cool

Bottle palm, Elephant's foot (*Beaucarnea recurvata*)

A tough windowsill plant with a woody stem which becomes very smooth at the base and is topped by graceful narrow-leaved arching foliage.

• water liberally in the summer but sparingly in winter; feed occasionally throughout the year
• repot in spring, using free-draining compost
• propagate by offsets in spring

low light, humid

Elatior begonia, Reiger begonia (*Begonia elatior*)

Fully double flowers in white, yellow, orange, pink and red are produced all year round on neat, fairly dwarf plants.

• water and feed regularly at all times, but take care not to overwater, especially in winter
• no repotting necessary; discard straggly plants
• propagate by stem cuttings, but best to buy new plants

low light, humid

Rex begonia (*Begonia rex*)

An evergreen with large leaves variously marked and veined in silver, cream, red, purple or copper. Plants tend to grow to one side.

• water and feed regularly in summer, keeping compost fairly moist in winter; in spring and summer spray daily with clear water
• repot every spring
• propagate by leaf cuttings in summer and autumn

bright light, warm

Bougainvillea (*Bougainvillea* hybrid)

A climber which produces coloured bracts during spring and summer.

• water freely in summer but keep almost dry in winter; feed regularly during the growing season
• repot in spring when young; older plants better top-dressed or repotted every other year; prune in early spring
• propagate by stem cuttings in spring and summer, but expect a low percentage of 'takes'

bright light, cool

Ornamental cabbage, Flowering cabbage (*Brassica oleracea*)

Plants with attractive leaves which often have finely cut edges. The variegated foliage is best in autumn and winter when temperatures are low.
• water and feed regularly during full growth, but keep on the drier side in winter
• discard before flowering in spring as plants become rather unkempt
• propagate by seed sown in summer

light, draughty

Common box (*Buxus sempervirens*)

An evergreen frost-hardy shrub attaining over 1m (3ft) in height even when grown in a container. The small roundish leaves emit a pungent smell.
• water and feed freely in the growing season; do not allow to become too dry at the root in winter
• clip to shape in spring and late summer
• repot in spring, but when grown in a large container top-dress the compost
• propagate by cuttings in spring or autumn

light, humid

Angels' wings, Elephant's ears (*Caladium* x *hortulanum*)

The leaves die back in winter to a tuber, which often proves difficult to keep. A temperature of 21°C (70°F) is needed to help commence growth in the spring.
• water regularly when in full growth; in winter keep the compost just moist; spray foliage daily
• pot tubers in spring
• propagate by removing offsets from the tubers

low light, humid

Calathea crocata

The dark green leaves have silvery markings and are pale purple beneath. The flower spike comprises orange flowers further enhanced by orange, or sometimes red, bracts which give a cone-like appearance.
• keep compost moist at all times and feed regularly, especially during spring and summer
• repot in spring
• propagate by division in spring

low light, cool

Slipper plant (*Calceolaria* x *herbeohybrida*)

Masses of pouch-shaped flowers are produced in spring. The compact foliage is soft and somewhat hairy.
• water freely during the growing season, and keep compost moist in winter; feed regularly
• discard plant after flowering
• propagate by seed in summer for flowering the following spring

bright light, cool

Bottlebrush plant (*Callistemon citrinus*)

The bottlebrush plant attains about 1m (3ft) in height and bears brilliant red flowers resembling bottle-brushes, which keep in good condition throughout the summer.
• water regularly in spring and summer, but keep drier in winter; feed fortnightly when in full growth
• repot in spring, using lime-free compost
• propagate by stem cuttings in early summer

low light, cool

Camellia (*Camellia japonica*)

Not the easiest plant for the home, but given cool airy conditions, and put outdoors in summer, it can achieve annual flowering in spring.

- water freely in spring and summer, but keep drier in winter; feed regularly during full growth; prune to shape after flowering
- repot in spring only as required
- propagate by stem or leaf cuttings in summer

bright light, cool

Bell flower (*Campanula isophylla*)

A trailing plant with white or blue star-like flowers borne on slender stems with downy greyish foliage. Other species are available with compact growth, bright green leaves and often fully double blooms.

- water well in spring and summer, reduce in winter; feed weekly when in full growth
- repot every year in early spring
- propagate by cuttings in spring

low light, humid

Dwarf mountain palm (*Chamaedorea elegans*)

A graceful slow-growing small palm. Bright green foliage is held on slightly arching main stems.

- water freely from spring to autumn; keep compost just moist in winter; feed every fortnight during the growing season
- repot every second year
- propagate by seed in spring, ensuring a high temperature up to 21°C (70°F)

bright light, warm

Chamaelaucium uncinatum

A shrubby plant with fine narrow leaves and small clusters of white, pink or lilac flowers, which are produced over a long period.

- water carefully at all times, especially in winter; feed fortnightly in spring and summer
- repot in spring, but do not choose too large a pot and use free-draining compost; lightly prune as necessary after flowering
- propagate by stem cuttings in summer

bright light, cool

European fan palm (*Chamaerops humilis*)

Although growing quite tall in the wild, this palm can be kept within bounds in pots. The greyish-green divided leaves are fan shaped and held on spiny stems.

- keep compost moist at all times, and feed every fortnight from spring to autumn
- repot every second year in spring
- propagate by suckers in spring

low light, cool
(needs bright light in winter)

Spider plant (*Chlorophytum comosum* 'Variegatum')

The foliage is green-and-white striped, and the arching flower stems have white star-like blooms.

- water and feed regularly during the growing season; water sparingly and give occasional feeds in winter
- repot in spring or summer
- propagate by division, or by separating the small stem-borne plants, and pot individually

bright light, cool

Chrysanthemum
(*Chrysanthemum* x *morifolium*)

A familiar flower, with only the specially grown plants suitable for indoors. Flowering can be had all year round, and its double or single flowers appear in many colours.

- water liberally when in flower; feed every two to three weeks
- discard plant after flowering
- best to buy new plants

low light, cool

Kangaroo vine (*Cissus antarctica*)

An easily grown climber which can be kept within bounds by pinching out the growing tips. The foliage is particularly decorative when young. Some support will be required.

- water moderately in spring and summer, sparingly in winter; feed regularly in spring and summer and reduce in winter
- repot every two years in spring
- propagate by leaf cuttings in spring or summer

bright light, cool

Calamondin orange
(x *Citrofortunella microcarpa*)

A bushy slow-growing evergreen bearing white, waxy fragrant flowers sporadically throughout the year, followed by tiny oranges.

- water moderately at all times, but keep a little drier in summer; feed from spring to summer; spray occasionally to ensure pollination
- repot as necessary in spring
- propagate by cuttings or seed in spring

bright light, warm

Bleeding heart vine
(*Clerodendrum thomsoniae*)

A fairly strong-growing evergreen climber which can be kept within bounds by pruning and twisting round a wire or cane frame.

- water regularly from spring to autumn and feed every fortnight; keep compost just moist in winter
- repot in spring if the root system is well developed; prune old growth back hard
- propagate by stem cuttings in spring

bright light, cool

Kaffir lily (*Clivia miniata*)

In spring orange-red trumpet-shaped flowers are borne on stiff stems which arise from a cluster of dark green strap-like leaves.

- feed sparingly and only water occasionally in summer; allow compost to dry out between each watering in the winter
- repot only when the plant becomes too congested in spring
- propagate by division after flowering

bright light, humid

Croton (*Codiaeum variegatum*)

An evergreen shrub whose leaves come in many shapes and colour combinations and require warmth and good light to intensify their brightness. Do not allow temperatures to fall below 13°C (55°F).

- water and feed regularly from spring to autumn; spray often throughout the year
- repot in spring
- propagate from stem cuttings

bright light, humid

Cabbage palm (*Cordyline australis*)

A shrub reaching at least 3m (10ft) when grown in its natural tropical habitat, but only attaining a third of that height in a 15cm (6in) pot.

• water freely from spring to autumn, moderately in winter; feed weekly during full growth

• repot in spring or summer

• propagate from basal shoots, tops of leggy plants or sections of bare stems; underground shoots can be separated and potted

bright light, warm

Jade plant, Money tree (*Crassula ovata*)

The Jade plant has compact tree-like growth with oval succulent leaves. Masses of starry flowers are produced in spring. Variegated and coloured-leaved forms are also available.

• water sparingly in spring and summer; keep dry at other times

• repot every year in spring

• propagate by stem cuttings or individual leaves in spring or summer

bright light, cool

Crocus (*Crocus vernus*)

There are many cultivated forms, with large, funnel-shaped to rounded, white, purple or blue flowers, which appear in early spring or autumn.

• water freely when in flower

• pot in autumn and keep in a cool, dark place to encourage root production

• after flowering discard old corms and plant outdoors

bright light, cool

Golden Monterey cypress (*Cupressus macrocarpa* 'Goldcrest')

An evergreen with fine leaves which assume a distinctly gold colour in good light. It is not reliably hardy.

• water and feed regularly during spring and summer; keep compost moist in autumn and winter

• repot in spring; prune to shape in summer

• propagate by heel cuttings in late summer

low light, cool

Cycad, Sago palm (*Cycas revoluta*)

Not a true palm but has similar growth, with stout fronds with many stiff leaflets arising from a short, almost ball-shaped base.

• keep compost moist at all times but avoid waterlogging; feed occasionally throughout the growing season

• repot every two to three years in spring or summer

• propagate in spring by removing side growths

low light, cool

Cyclamen (*Cyclamen persicum*)

Hybrid cultivars have white, pink, red or crimson flowers, and many have marked foliage.

• keep compost moist when in full growth; feed every fortnight when in flower; spray daily with water; allow compost to dry out and place on its side outdoors in late spring; carefully remove dead flowers and leaf stems in their entirety

• repot every summer when new growth appears

• propagate by seed in late summer

low light, cool/warm

Cymbidium (*Cymbidium* hybrid)

Cymbidium varieties are some of the easiest orchids to grow, and and they remain healthy in ordinary room conditions.

• keep compost moist by reduced watering in winter; feed every two to three weeks; use soft water; spray in spring and summer
• repot occasionally when plants deteriorate; use special orchid compost
• propagate by division

low light, cool

Umbrella grass (*Cyperus alternifolius*)

The green foliage is formed into tufts like umbrella frames on top of fairly stiff stems up to 60cm (2ft) high.

• keep well watered at all times, even standing it in a water-filled shallow container; feed weekly from spring to autumn
• repot in spring
• propagate by division or seed; the 'umbrella' will also root in winter

low light, cool

Dumb cane (*Dieffenbachia compacta*)

There are many forms, all with attractively marked foliage which is, however, poisonous. Occasionally rather inconspicuous greenish flowers are formed.

• keep compost moist at all times and feed fortnightly from spring to autumn
• repot every spring
• propagate by division, stem cuttings or stem section in spring or summer

bright light, cool

Madagascar dragon tree (*Dracaena marginata* 'Colorama')

A slow-growing species, whose tough narrow leaves are dark green with cream and pink stripes.

• water regularly in spring and summer, reducing at the start of winter; feed once every two weeks during growing period
• repot every other spring
• propagate by stem sections or tip cuttings

bright light, cool

Mexican gem, Mexican snow ball (*Echeveria elegans*)

A succulent plant with fleshy foliage formed in a rosette. The erect flower stem has pinkish blooms with yellow inside which appear in spring and summer.

• water sparingly at all times, especially in winter and feed monthly from spring to late summer
• repot every second year in spring
• propagate from offsets or leaf cuttings

bright light, warm

Abyssinian banana (*Ensete ventricosum* 'Maurellii')

A banana plant bearing inedible fruit but with attractive maroon-blotched green leaves. Growing to about 1.6m (5½ft), it has a spread of a similar measurement.

• water and feed regularly in spring and summer, but keep compost almost dry in winter
• repot in spring
• propagate by division in spring

low light, humid

Devil's ivy (*Epipremnum aureum*)

A fairly strong-growing climber, but can be kept within bounds in a container and supported on a framework. The mature leaves are heart-shaped, green splashed with golden yellow.
• water and feed regularly during the growing season but keep compost just moist in winter
• repot every second year in spring; pinch growths to encourage bushiness
• propagate by section of stem with one leaf

bright light, cool

Blue gum (*Eucalyptus gunnii*)

The blue-grey foliage is very aromatic when crushed and changes from oval to a longer, narrower shape with age. It is fast growing, and ultimately requires a larger container.
• water and feed liberally from spring to autumn; keep compost moist in winter
• repot in spring and cut back hard to retain young foliage on new growth
• propagate by seed sown in spring

low light, cool

Japanese spindle tree (*Euonymus fortunei*)

A bushy shrub with evergreen foliage, the variegated forms being the most attractive. The species *E. fortunei* is compact and often trailing, and therefore suitable for edging.
• water regularly, especially in dry conditions; feed fortnightly
• repot in spring
• propagate by stem cuttings in summer

bright light, warm

Poinsettia (*Euphorbia pulcherrima*)

The insignificant flowers are surrounded by large coloured bracts in winter. Plants with red, white, pink and variegated bracts are available.
• keep compost moist when in full growth and feed fortnightly; after flowering keep compost dry, and stand plant outdoors in a sheltered spot in late spring; spray daily with clear water
• repot and prune back hard in summer
• propagate by stem cuttings in summer

low light, cool

Fat-headed lizzie, Ivy tree (*Fatshedera lizei*)

This semi-climbing evergreen will need some support, although with careful pinching and pruning a shorter plant can be produced.
• water and feed regularly from spring to autumn, but be careful not to over-water
• repot in spring
• propagate from stem cuttings in spring or autumn

bright light, draughty, cool

False castor-oil plant, Fig leaf palm (*Fatsia japonica*)

A fast-growing plant reaching well over 2m (6ft) and half as much across. The large glossy leaves help make this a bold and impressive specimen.
• water and feed freely from spring to autumn; keep compost moist and feed occasionally during winter
• repot in spring
• propagate by stem cuttings in summer

low light, warm

Weeping fig (*Ficus benjamina*)

A popular plant for entrance halls, making a medium-sized tree naturally but growing to about 2m (6ft) indoors in a large container.

• keep compost moist at all times and feed regularly from spring to autumn; wipe the leaves with a damp sponge but avoid scarring

• repot in spring, or cut back hard and subsequently select a suitable growth to repot

• propagate by tip or leafbud cuttings in summer

bright light, cool

Kumquat (*Fortunella margarita*)

A tree-like evergreen growing to about 1m (3ft) in a pot. Clusters of white scented flowers appear in spring and summer, followed by small edible orange fruits which ripen in autumn and winter.

• water and feed regularly except in winter, but even then keep compost moist

• repot in early spring every year

• propagate by stem cuttings

bright light, cool

Strawberry (*Fragaria* x *ananassa*)

A well-known fruiting plant that adapts to growing in pots, with certain cultivars suitable for hanging baskets.

• water and feed regularly in spring and summer; keep compost moist in winter

• propagate by rooting runners in small pots in summer having placed the parent plant outdoors. Discard after propagation. Raise hanging basket types from seed sown in spring

low light, cool

Snowdrop (*Galanthus nivalis*)

The white pendant flowers open in mid- and late winter. There are many forms, including fully double cultivars.

• keep compost moist when in full growth and feed every fortnight

• Pot in autumn, although dry bulbs can give indifferent results; after flowering grow on as plants outdoors; the bulbs normally increase well so that clumps can be divided

low light, warm

Gardenia, Cape jasmine (*Gardenia augusta*)

The double, heavily scented flowers are held on fairly compact plants with evergreen foliage.

• water freely in summer but sparingly in winter; feed fortnightly; buds often fall as an indication of over- or under-watering; spray regularly with clear water

• repot every two years in spring and summer

• propagate by seed in spring

bright light, cool

Silk bark oak (*Grevillea robusta*)

This is really an Australian tree, but in its early years it is attractive as a single specimen or a background subject.

• water and feed liberally in the growing season; keep compost moist in winter; excessive heat, dry atmosphere or over-watering can lead to leaf fall

• repot in spring, or cut back hard and select one or several new growths to repot

• propagate by seed in spring or summer

low light, draughty, cool

Common ivy (*Hedera helix*)

An evergreen climber or trailer with many forms, either variegated or with diverse leaf shape.

• keep soil moist and feed regularly during the growing season; wipe foliage with damp sponge

• repot in spring

• prune back hard to produce new growth on old plant; remove all growth if leaves are changing character; pinch shoots to train in required form

• propagate by cuttings in summer and autumn

bright light, cool

Sunflower (*Helianthus annuus*)

Very dwarf forms, suitable for pot culture, are now available. Although not flowering over a long period, they are quite spectacular and of interest to children.

• keep watered in the growing season and feed every week

• discard when flowering is over

• propagate by seed sown in spring or early summer

bright light, humid

**Rose of China
(*Hibiscus rosa-sinensis*)**

An evergreen shrub with large flowers coloured from white through yellow to pink and red. Hybrids bred for the home are compact.

• water and feed regularly during spring and summer; keep compost just moist at all times; spray daily with clear water

• repot in spring and prune to shape

• propagate by stem cuttings

bright light, cool

Amaryllis (*Hippeastrum* hybrid)

Large trumpet-shaped flowers are held on stiff erect stems which rise from a bulb. The many hybrids are available in a wide range of colours.

• water freely, especially when foliage appears; feed weekly when in full flower and leaf; keep dry when foliage dies back; put bulb in full sun after flowering

• repot or top dress every two to three years

• propagate by offsets

low light, warm

Curly palm (*Howea belmoreana*)

Similar in many ways to the Kentia palm (see right), but the fronds are held on fairly stiff stems which bend over.

• water liberally from spring to autumn, then more sparingly; feed fortnightly in spring and summer, and monthly for the rest of the year

• repot every other year in spring; cut off dead fronds as near to the main stem as possible

• propagate by seed in spring in warmth

low light, warm

Kentia palm (*Howea forsteriana*)

Although growing quite tall, it stays in good condition and a manageable size for many years. The graceful fronds comprise several long leaflets.

• water liberally from spring to autumn and sparingly in the winter; feed fortnightly

• repot every two years in spring; as fronds die, cut off at the base as near to the main stem as possible

• propagate by seed in spring

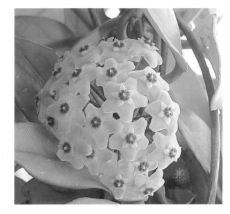

bright light, warm

Wax flower (*Hoya carnosa*)

A climbing plant with thick evergreen foliage and clusters of honey-scented flowers borne from spring to autumn. Train on a cane or wire frame. Do not remove old stems as new flowers are produced from these the following year.
• water freely in summer but sparingly at other times; feed fortnightly when in flower
• repot in spring every second year
• propagate by stem cuttings in summer

bright light, cool

Hyacinth (*Hyacinthus orientalis*)

Very fragrant flowers in pink, red, white and purple. Roman hyacinths are multi-stemmed. Specially prepared bulbs can be forced into flower by Christmas.
• water and feed liberally when in growth
• pot in autumn but do not totally bury bulbs; prior to forcing keep bulbs dark and cool to make a good root system; remove into full light when growth is about 5cm (2in)

low light, cool

Hydrangea (*Hydrangea hortensis*)

'Mop-head' or 'lace-cap' types have flower-heads in white, pink, red or blue, the latter induced by the application to the soil of a special colorant.
• keep compost quite moist during full growth and feed every week; reduce watering in winter
• repot every spring and prune back hard to plumb-based buds
• propagate by stem cuttings in spring

low light, cool

Busy lizzy, New Guinea Hybrid (*Impatiens hawkeri*)

A popular plant with large flowers, in a wide range of colours held on neat plants with dark and sometimes colourfully variegated foliage.
• water regularly from spring to autumn; keep compost moist but not waterlogged in winter; feed every week during the growing season
• repot in spring, but best to discard
• propagate by stem cuttings

low light (in summer only), cool

Slender club rush (*Isolepis cernua*)

A very fine-leaved grass-like plant with long blades that curve over the pot as they grow. Its graceful outline complements bolder-leaved plants; it is also effective in hanging baskets.
• keep well watered and fed during the growing season; do not allow to dry out during winter as the plant is semi-aquatic
• repot in spring
• propagate by division

bright light, cool

Jasmine (*Jasminum polyanthum*)

A vigorous climber that can be kept within bounds by cutting back hard after flowering and training subsequent growths on a wire support.
• keep compost moist at all times; increase watering prior to flowering; feed weekly from spring to late summer
• repot in spring, or discard if growth is too rampant at the expense of the flower
• propagate by stem cuttings in spring or summer

bright light, cool

Tom Thumb (*Kalanchoe blossfeldiana* hybrids)

This leafy free-flowering succulent produces starry five-petalled flowers in clusters. The flowers come in white, pink, orange and red and are available in bloom all year.

• water freely in summer but sparingly in winter; feed fortnightly from spring to autumn
• repot in spring or discard
• propagate by seed or cuttings in spring

bright light, cool

Bay tree, Sweet bay, True laurel (*Lauris nobilis*)

An evergreen bush whose aromatic leaves are used for culinary purposes. It makes a good topiary subject for large containers.

• water regularly from spring to autumn but sparingly in winter; feed weekly during the growing season
• repot or top-dress in spring; prune in summer
• propagate by stem cuttings in summer

bright light, cool

French lavender (*Lavandula stoechas*)

This lavender has prominently winged flowers and comes in a range of colours from white through pink to deep blue. It is best kept in a porch, and should be moved outdoors during the summer.

• water and feed regularly during spring and summer; keep compost just moist in winter
• repot in spring
• propagate by cuttings in autumn

bright light, cool

Tea tree (*Leptospermum scoparium*)

A fairly fine-leaved evergreen shrub producing white, pink, red, crimson or cerise flowers in summer. Larger hybrids are best grown in tubs in the conservatory.

• water and feed regularly from spring to autumn; keep compost just moist in winter
• repot in spring using a free-draining compost
• propagate by stem cuttings in summer or sow seed in autumn or spring

low light, cool

Easter lily (*Lilium longiflorum*)

Although it can be forced into flower in spring its natural flowering time is summer. Heavily scented, white trumpet-shaped flowers are borne on 1m (3ft) stems.

• water liberally when in full growth; feed every week; after flowering keep compost moist
• repot bulb in autumn
• propagate by offsets when repotting, or by seed in autumn or spring

bright light, cool

Powder puff (*Mammillaria prolifera* var. *texana*)

There are many species of this free-flowering cacti which often have lightly coloured fruits. Keep plants turned regularly to avoid lopsided growth.

• water regularly in spring and summer, but keep compost quite dry in winter; give monthly feeds
• repot in spring using a fine-grained compost
• propagate by seed in spring or offsets in summer

low light, warm

Rose grape (*Medinilla magnifica*)

A plant with prominently veined leathery leaves. The long-lasting flowers are rose-pink and purple, with pink bracts clustered on pendulous stems.

• water freely from spring to summer but more sparingly in winter; spray regularly with clear water; feed weekly during the growing season and reduce in winter

• repot every other year in spring

• propagate by stem cuttings in spring or summer

bright light, cool

Mint, Spearmint (*Mentha spicata*)

A well-known herb which can be pot-grown indoors, especially for early and late culinary use. Bell-shaped flowers appear in summer.

• water liberally from spring to autumn, but greatly reduce in winter; feed regularly when in full growth

• repot every spring; pinch out flower heads

• propagate by division in spring, cuttings in spring or summer

low light, warm

Sensitive plant (*Mimosa pudica*)

The feathery leaves instantly fold and droop when touched – hence the name – but spread again after about half an hour. Fluffy pink ball-like clusters of tiny flowers are produced in spring and autumn.

• water carefully, keeping compost moist; feed fortnightly; spray with clear water

• discard when the plant deteriorates in autumn

• propagate by seed sown in spring

low light, humid

Swiss cheese plant (*Monstera deliciosa*)

A climbing plant with evergreen shield-shaped leaves. Occasionally creamy-white arum-like flowers appear, followed by a delicious fruit.

• water and feed liberally during spring and summer, keeping compost moist at other times

• repot every two to three years; cut back old straggly plants hard in spring

• propagate by stem or leaf cuttings in summer

bright light, cool

Myrtle (*Myrtus communis*)

An evergreen shrub with aromatic foliage and fluffy white scented flowers from spring to autumn. A variegated form is available.

• water regularly in spring and summer, sparingly in winter; feed weekly when in full growth

• repot in spring

• in summer move outdoors to a sheltered sunny spot

• propagate by cuttings in summer

bright light, cool

Narcissus, Daffodil (*Narcissus* spp.)

These flowers can be forced into early flowering, with cultivars capable of blooming by Christmas.

• keep moist at all times and feed weekly when in full growth; place outdoors after flowering

• pot several bulbs in autumn, and when required for forcing keep bulbs dark and cool, to encourage rooting, prior to bringing into warmer conditions to flower; bulbs will not be suitable for flowering indoors the following year

low light, cool

Boston fern (*Nephrolepis exaltata*)

There are many forms of this attractive long-lived fern, all of which may be grown in pots. The normal species has stiff fronds, but some cultivars have feathery, arching or twisted ones.
• water freely in spring and summer, keeping compost just moist at all other times; feed every fortnight when in full growth
• repot in spring every second year
• propagate by division

bright light, cool

Nerine (*Nerine* spp.)

There are many hybrids of this beautiful autumn-flowering bulb. The flower-heads are held on erect stems 0.6m (2ft) high. Colours range from white or pink to red or orange.
• Commence watering when leaves appear; feed fortnightly; keep dry when bulb is dormant
• repot every three years in summer; do not bury the bulb
• propagate by offsets when potting on

bright light, cool

Oleander (*Nerium oleander*)

A plant requiring plenty of room to grow. It makes bushy growths with evergreen narrow leaves and clusters of flowers, usually pink. All parts of the plant are poisonous.
• water regularly in spring and summer, but much more sparingly in winter; feed weekly during the growing season
• repot when necessary in spring; prune in autumn
• propagate by stem cuttings in summer

bright light, cool

Basil (*Ocimum basilicum*)

This aromatic annual or semi-perennial herb has shiny bright green or deep purple, sometimes slightly hairy, leaves. The flower-heads, usually white but occasionally pinky-purple, are quite attractive but can be removed to encourage bushiness.
• water and feed regularly in summer
• discard in autumn
• propagate by seed in spring

bright light, cool

Olive (*Olea europea*)

Only suitable for growing in a conservatory or glazed corridor where its evergreen, somewhat dull green-silvery foliage makes a useful contribution, especially in dry-air conditions. White flowers may be formed after several years.
• water and feed regularly from spring to autumn, and reduce both in winter
• repot or top-dress every year
• propagate by stem cuttings in summer

bright light, cool

Sweet marjoram (*Origanum majorana*)

An upright evergreen plant with a culinary use but also quite decorative, with its dull green leaves enhanced by white or pink flowers held in clusters.
• water liberally during summer and give weekly feeds
• discard in autumn
• propagate by seeds in spring

bright light, cool

Passion flower (*Passiflora caerulea*)

A climbing plant whose large blue-and-white flowers appear from summer to autumn. The yellow-flowered species *P. citrina* is less rampant.

• water liberally in spring and summer, and keep compost moist in winter; feed regularly

• repot in early spring every other year; prune back hard in spring; twine growth to support

• propagate by stem cuttings in summer or seed in spring

bright light, warm

**Regal pelargonium
(*Pelargonium* x *domesticum*)**

'Regals' have a shorter flowering season than geraniums but are more flamboyant. The single, occasionally double, flowers appear in clusters.

• water freely when in full growth; keep compost just moist when not in flower

• repot as necessary in spring

• propagate by stem cuttings in spring, summer or autumn

bright light, warm

Geranium (*Pelargonium* x *hortorum*)

Long-lasting flowering plants with 'geraniums' often have highly coloured or zoned foliage. White, pink, red and purple single or double flowers are available in this and 'regal'.

• water freely when in full growth; keep compost just moist when not in flower

• repot as necessary in spring

• propagate by stem cuttings in spring, summer or autumn

bright light, cool

**Egyptian star cluster
(*Pentas lanceolata*)**

Recently introduced dwarf forms are becoming popular as long-lasting flowering subjects. The hairy-leaved stems terminate in clusters of starry flowers in white, pink or red.

• water and feed regularly from spring to autumn; keep compost just moist in winter

• repot in early spring or discard

• propagate by seed or stem cuttings in spring

low light, cool

Cineraria (*Pericallis* x *hybrida*)

Daisy-like flowers are formed into a large head over heart-shaped leaves. They come in a wide colour range in winter and spring.

• water carefully at all times, keeping compost just moist especially in winter; feed every two weeks whilst flowering continues; spray with clear water

• discard after flowering

• propagate by seed in summer

low light, cool/warm

Moth orchid (*Phalaenopsis* hybrid)

Phalaenopsis hybrids are some of the most accommodating of orchids. The flowers appear twice a year and remain in bloom for months.

• keep compost moist throughout the year; use soft water; feed every two to three weeks

• repot when plants deteriorate, using special orchid compost

• propagate by rooting plantlets formed on the flower stems

low light, humid

Heart-leaf philodendron
(*Philodendron scandens*)

A climber with heart-shaped leaves. The slender stems intertwine but need a strong support. Pinch to encourage bushiness.
• keep compost moist in winter and early spring, otherwise water regularly; feed fortnightly during the growing season
• repot in spring or summer every second year
• propagate by stem cuttings

bright light, humid
(avoid direct sunlight in summer)

Pygmy date palm (*Phoenix roebelinii*)

A slow-growing graceful palm. Although ultimately reaching 2m (6ft), it makes an ideal house plant.
• water freely in spring and summer, and feed fortnightly; keep compost moist at other times and feed monthly
• pot initially every year, then every two to three years in spring
• propagate by seed which should be pre-soaked for 24 hours in warm water in spring

bright light, cool

Mock orange, Tobira
(*Pittosporum tobira*)

An evergreen shrub growing to about 2m (6ft) in a large container. Variegated and compact forms are available. The orange-scented creamy flowers appear in spring and summer.
• water and feed liberally in spring and summer; keep compost moist in winter
• repot in spring as required
• propagate by stem cuttings in summer

low light, cool

Swedish ivy (*Plectranthus*)

A trailing plant and therefore ideal for hanging baskets. The foliage is dull green with silvery veins above and purple below. Pale-violet flower spikes appear late winter to spring.
• keep compost moist at all times, watering and feeding freely from spring to autumn
• repot in spring
• propagate by cuttings in spring or summer, or by division in spring

bright light, cool

Cape leadwort (*Plumbago capensis*)

An open-growing shrubby plant which can easily be kept within bounds by hard pruning in spring. Clear blue flowers appear from early summer to autumn. A white form is available.
• water freely in the growing season, and keep compost just moist in winter; feed regularly
• repot as necessary in spring
• propagate by stems cuttings in autumn and seed in spring

low light, cool

Miniature bamboo
(*Pogonatherum panaceum*)

A recent introduction, forming many dwarf-stemmed clustered growths with broad grass-like bright-green foliage. Smooth, usually hollow canes produce stems at each node.
• water and feed freely in summer; keep compost moist at all other times
• repot in spring
• propagate by division in spring

low light, cool

Poison primrose (*Primula obconica*)

The unfortunately named primula refers to the leaves that can cause a skin rash on susceptible people. However, new hybrids have been bred to eliminate the irritant in the sap. Flowers are produced almost continuously.

• keep compost moist at all times; feed every two weeks

• repot in late spring

• propagate by seed in spring and summer

bright light, cool

Azalea (*Rhododendron simsii*)

A compact bush with evergreen leaves and a mass of flowers opening naturally in spring. However, the plant can be forced into flower much earlier. Stand outdoors in summer.

• water freely with soft water, keeping the compost moist in winter; be careful of waterlogging; feed regularly; spray often

• repot in lime-free compost after flowering

• propagate by stem cuttings in summer

bright light, cool

Rose (*Rosa* hybrids)

These miniature shrubs are scaled-down versions of typical garden roses in a wide range of colours, all with double flowers. Remove dead flowers as they appear.

• water and feed regularly from spring to autumn, but keep compost just moist in winter

• repot in spring and prune back growth that flowered the previous year; also plant outdoors

• propagate by cuttings in summer

bright light, cool

Rosemary (*Rosmarinus officinalis*)

The aromatic plant has many forms and is grown as a culinary herb or decorative flowering plant. Not really suitable as a house plant, but useful in a large porch.

• water regularly and feed weekly in spring and summer

• repot or top-dress weekly in spring and summer

• propagate by cuttings in autumn

low light, humid

African violet (*Saintpaulia ionantha*)

Long-lasting violet flowers appear in the centre of a rosette of velvety, heart-shaped leaves. White, pink, blue and purple single and double forms are available.

• keep compost moist at all times, always using tepid water, and avoid wetting the leaves; feed every two to three weeks in spring and summer

• repot every two years in spring

• propagate by leaf cuttings or seed in spring

bright light, cool

Christmas cactus (*Schlumbergera x buckleyi*)

The stems are flat and leaf-like, with the pendant or erect trumpet-shaped white, pink, orange or red flowers produced at their tips in winter.

• water and feed freely in spring and summer; keep out of direct sun in summer, but give good light conditions in winter

• repot in spring every second year

• propagate by cuttings in summer

low light, cool

Queensland umbrella tree
(*Schefflera actinophylla* 'Nova')
An upright evergreen, with various cultivars
having variegation to a greater or lesser degree.
• water and feed regularly in spring and
summer, gradually decreasing in autumn and
keeping compost just moist in winter
• repot in spring; cut back hard in spring if plant
has become leggy but do not then repot
• propagate by stem cuttings in summer

low light, cool

False aralia, Finger aralia
(*Schefflera elegantissima*)
Best when young, as the notched finger-like
leaves become coarse and less attractive with age.
• water carefully in winter but keep compost
moist in spring and summer; feed regularly
• repot in spring, but when the plant becomes
leggy cut back the main stem to encourage
new shoots – do not repot then
• propagate by seed in spring

low light, warm

Spreading club moss
(*Selaginella kraussiana*)
A fern-like moss with spreading low-growing
stems which are much branched with yellowish
green-tinged leaves.
• water regularly in spring and summer, and
give occasional feeds; water sparingly in winter;
spray regularly with water during growing season
• repot in spring
• propagate by cuttings in spring or summer

bright light, cool

Skimmia (*Skimmia japonica* 'Rubella')
A bushy evergreen with fragrant white flowers
which are pink in the bud. The flowers stems
are reddish-bronze and are decorative even
before blossoming.
• keep compost moist at all times; feed
fortnightly in spring and summer
• repot every year in spring
• propagate by stem cuttings in summer or
sow seed in cold frame in autumn

bright light, cool

Winter cherry (*Solanum capsicastrum*)
Grown for its orange-red berries which ripen in
late autumn and winter. The shrubby stems
have dark-green foliage, with white star-like
flowers appearing in summer.
• keep compost moist at all times and feed
every fortnight; spray daily
• repot and prune to shape in spring; stand
outdoors in summer
• propagate by seed or stem cuttings in spring

low light, draughty

**Baby's tears, Irish moss, Mind your
own business** (*Soleirolia soleirolii*)
A compact plant in general, but capable of
spreading over quite a large area and therefore
useful for covering the surfaces of pots with single
subjects. Golden and white variegated forms are
available, but the leaves often revert to pale green.
• keep moist at all times; do not overfeed
• repot from spring to autumn
• propagate by division from spring to autumn

bright light, humid

Flame nettle, Coleus
(*Solenostemon scutellariodes*)

A very variable plant in leaf form, colour and size, which can reach between 30 and 60cm (1–2ft).

• water freely in summer but keep soil just moist in winter; feed weekly in spring and summer

• repotting each year is not worth doing for mature plants, as young plants are best propagated regularly by cuttings from spring to autumn or seed sown in spring

low light, cool

House lime, African hemp
(*Sparrmannia africana*)

A shrub with pale green, downy leaves and white flowers with prominent stamens, which expand rapidly when touched.

• water well in spring and summer, and reduce in winter; feed weekly from spring to summer

• repot or top-dress in spring; prune back hard after flowering

• propagate by stem cuttings in spring

low light, cool

Peace lily (*Sphathiphyllum wallisii*)

Although this plant has attractive glossy-green foliage the pure white arum-shaped inflorescences which appear in spring add to its decorativeness.

• keep compost moist at all times; feed every two weeks from spring to autumn, and monthly in winter

• repot every spring

• propagate by division in spring

bright light, warm
(cool in winter)

Madagascar jasmine
(*Stephanotis floribunda*)

A climber with very fragrant white waxy flowers. Training on a support is essential.

• water freely from spring to autumn, keeping compost just moist in winter; spray regularly in summer; feed regularly in spring and summer

• repot every two years in spring; cut back after flowering

• propagate by stem cuttings in summer

low light, warm

Cape cowslip, Cape primrose
(*Streptocarpus* x hybrid)

From spring to autumn, white, pink, red, blue or purple trumpet-shaped flowers are held on wiry stems above a rosette of foliage.

• water and feed freely during full growth, but sparingly in winter

• repot every year in spring in a shallow pot

• propagate by leaf cuttings in summer, seed or division in spring

bright light, cool

Black-eyed Susan (*Thunbergia alata*)

A fast-growing climbing plant with slender stems that readily intertwine but require good support. The yellow flowers have dark chocolate-coloured centres and appear from late spring to autumn.

• keep watered and fed regularly when in full growth

• Treat as an annual and discard after flowering

bright light, cool

Thyme (*Thymus vulgaris* 'Aureus')

This popular culinary herb is a small evergreen perennial. Several variegated forms are particularly decorative. Small mauve flowers appear in summer.

- water and feed regularly in spring and summer, and sparingly at other times, being careful to avoid waterlogging
- repot every spring; prune annually to keep shape
- propagate by division or cuttings in spring

low light, cool
(bright light in winter)

Speedy Jenny (*Tradescantia fluminensis* 'Variegata')

It is the variegated forms of this plant that are really decorative. Ideal for hanging baskets.

- water freely at all times, keeping compost moist in winter; feed fortnightly in spring and summer
- repot in spring as necessary; prune shoots to keep shapeliness, and remove all green reverted growth from the variegated forms
- propagate by cuttings from spring to autumn

bright light, cool

Tulip (*Tulipa* spp)

Many hundreds of cultivars exist, but the dwarf early-flowering forms are best for indoors. The cup-shaped flowers come in a wide range of colours, and some have attractively marked foliage.

- water liberally when in growth
- pot several bulbs in a container in autumn; keep in a cool dark place until growth appears, then move into full light

bright or low light, cool

Pansy (*Viola* x *wittrockiana*)

A popular flowering plant which produces blooms over a long period. The flowers come in a wide range of colours, including white, yellow, orange and blue, often with a contrasting 'face'.

- water and feed regularly from spring to autumn; keep compost moist in winter
- discard plants after flowering which may last for two years
- propagate by seed sown in spring or summer

bright light, cool

Spineless yucca (*Yucca elephantipes*)

Many sword-shaped leaves arise from a stout stem, giving an exotic palm-like appearance. Yuccas can last for years if treated with care. This spineless species is perfect for positioning in a hallway.

- water liberally in spring and summer, and much less often in winter; feed occasionally
- repot every year in spring
- propagate by offsets when repotting

bright light, cool

Arum lily (*Zantedeschia aethiopica*)

Although some forms can make quite large plants, dwarf varieties are available. The large green arrow-shaped leaves are held on thickish stems, with flower stems growing taller.

- water and feed liberally throughout the growing season, but reduce as foliage dies down, keeping compost just moist
- repot in autumn
- propagate by offshoots

SUPPLIERS

ALEXANDRA PALACE
GARDEN CENTRE
Alexandra Palace Way,
London N22 4BB
tel 020 8444 2555

ANGEL FLOWERS
Upper Street, Islington,
London N1 0NY
tel 020 7704 6312

THE CHELSEA GARDENER
125 Sydney Street,
London SW3 6NR
tel 020 7352 5656

CLIFTON NURSERIES
5a Clifton Villas, Little Venice,
London W9 2PH
tel 020 7289 6851

EUROPLANTS
Great North Road,
Bellbar, nr Hatfield,
Hertfordshire AL9 6DA
tel 01707 649996

THE HOLDING COMPANY
tel 020 7610 9160

PAULA PRYKE
20 Penton Street, Islington,
London N1 9PS
tel 020 7837 7336

THE PLANT ROOM
47 Barnsbury Street, Islington,
London N1 1TP
tel 020 7700 6766

THE ROMANTIC
GARDEN NURSERY
The Street, Swannington,
Norwich, Norfolk NR9 5NW
tel 01603 261488

SAINSBURY'S HOMEBASE
(various branches)
Head office tel 020 8784 7200

TAVERHAM NURSERY CENTRE
Fircovert Road, Taverham,
Norwich, Norfolk NR8 6HT
tel 01603 860522

WOODHAMS AT ONE ALDWYCH
One Aldwych,
London WC2 4BZ
tel 020 7300 0777

WYEVALE GARDEN CENTRE
Lower Morden Lane, Morden,
Surrey SM4 4SJ
tel 020 8337 7781

**Containers from most of the
above and:**
GEORGE CARTER
for Versailles cases

THE CONRAN SHOP
Michelin House, 81 Fulham Road,
London SW3 6RD
tel 020 7589 7401

HABITAT
tel 08456 010740

ORIEL HARWOOD'S vases and urns
are available from
David Gill, 60 Fulham Road,
London SW3 0HH
tel 020 7589 5946

HEALS
196 Tottenham Court Road,
London W1P 9LD
tel 020 7636 1666

MYRIAD ANTIQUES
131 Portland Road,
London W11 4LW
tel 020 7229 1709

WHICHFORD POTTERY
Whichford, nr Shipston-on-Stour,
Warwickshire CV36 5PG
tel 01608 684416

DESIGNERS AND ARCHITECTS

DORRINGTON PROPERTIES PLC
14 Hans Road,
London SW3 1RT
tel 020 7581 1477

ALASTAIR HOWE ARCHITECTS
50 Tanners Way, Hunsdon Ware,
Hertfordshire SG12 8QF
tel 01279 843936

JUSTIN MEATH BAKER
Baker Neville Design Partnership,
7 Barlow Place, Bruton Lane,
London W1X 7AE
tel 020 7491 9900

FLEUR ROSSDALE
THE INTERIOR DESIGN HOUSE
8 Avenue Crescent,
London W3 8EW
tel 020 8752 8648

BARBARA WEISS ARCHITECTS
4 Offord Street
London N1 1DH
tel 020 7609 1867

LOCATIONS

THE AMERICAN MUSEUM
IN BRITAIN
Claverton Manor,
Bath BA2 7BD
tel 01225 460503

HOTEL TRESANTON
St Mawes, Cornwall TR2 5DR
tel 01326 270055

INDEX

ACKNOWLEDGMENTS

The author and the publisher would like to thank everyone who generously allowed their interiors to be photographed: The American Museum in Britain, Bill McNaught and Judith Elsdon, Mr and Mrs David Cargill, Viscount and Viscountess Coke, Carol Davidson, Major and Mrs Charles Fenwick, Leslie Geddes-Brown and Hugh Stevenson, Mr and Mrs Nick Green, Oriel Harwood, Alastair Howe, Marianne Majerus and Robert Clark, Justin Meath Baker, Lysander Meath Baker, the Hon. Olga Polizzi and the Hon. William Shawcross, The Hotel Tresanton, Fleur Rossdale, Dawna Walter, Barbara Weiss, and Mr and Mrs Richard Winch.

The author would also like to thank Alison Starling whose idea this book was, Selina Mumford, Helen Taylor and Penny Warren at Mitchell Beazley, and especially Marianne Majerus, the photographer and her assistants Stewart Williams and Nicholas Clark-Majerus. And thanks to those who supplied plants for the photography including The Chelsea Gardener, Clifton Nurseries, The Romantic Garden Nursery and Angel Flowers. Finally, many thanks to Ray Waite for all his work on the plant directory.

PHOTO ACKNOWLEDGMENTS

Jacket photography: © Octopus Publishing Group Ltd/Marianne Majerus front jacket, back jacket, back jacket flap.
Octopus Publishing Group Ltd/Marianne Majerus 1, 2–3, 5, 10–11, 12, 12–13, 14, 15, 16–17, 19, 20, 21t, 21b, 23, 24t, 24b, 25, 27t, 27b, 28, 28–29, 29, 31, 32, 33t, 33b, 34, 35, 36, 37, 38, 38–39, 40–41,42, 43, 45, 48t, 48b, 50, 50–51, 53t, 53b, 54–55, 56, 57t, 58t, 58b, 60–61, 63, 64t, 64b, 66–67, 67, 68–69, 70t, 70b, 73, 74, 76, 77t, 77b, 78, 78–79, 80, 81, 83, 84–85, 86, 87, 88, 89, 90, 91, 92, 93, 94t, 94b, 95, 99t, 99b, 100, 101t, 101b, 105, 106, 107, 108, 109, 112l, 112tc, 112bl, 112br, 113tl, 113tr, 114tl, 114tc, 114bl, 114bc, 115tl, 119bl
Abode 18, 64–65, 72–73, 110–111; AKG London 8–9b; A–Z Botanical Collection 114tr, 116br, 123tr, 125tc, 131tr; Deni Bown Associates 127br; The Bridgeman Art Library/Mallet & Son Antiques Ltd, London/National Gallery, London 6b; Eric Crichton 114br, 118tr, 119tl, 120tr, 124tr, 124br, 125bl, 126bc, 127bc, 129br, 131tc, 131br; Derek St Romaine 121tc, 129bc; Garden Picture Library/Chris Burrows 132tr/Rex Butcher 117bc/Sunniva Harte 117tr/Neil Holmes 130bl, 130bc/A.I. Lord 126tr/Jerry Pavia 112tr/Howard Rice 116tc, 121tl, 132bl/JS Sira 112bc, 116bl, 117bl/Friedrich Strauss 115bl, 132br/Brigitte Thomas 113bc/Steven Wooster 115tr; John Glover 122tr, 122br, 132tl; Harpur Garden Library/Jerry Harpur 113tc, 117tl, 122tl, 129tc/Marcus Harpur 124bc; International Interiors/Paul Ryan 52, 62–63; The Interior Archive/Tim Beddow 82–83/Cecilia Innes 71/Fritz von der Schulenburg Endpapers, 22, 26, 30, 49, 74–75,102–103/Simon Upton 104; IPC Syndication/Country Homes and Interiors 59/Christopher Drake/Homes & Gardens 98 /Andreas von Einsiedel/Homes & Gardens 57br; Andrew Lawson Photography 115tc, 121tr, 124bl; Mainstream/Ray Main 96–97; National Museum, Copenhagen 8t; National Trust Photographic Llibrary/Derrick E. Witty 6–7t; Clive Nichols Garden Pictures 116bc; Photos Horticultural 116tr, 120bl, 121bc, 123br, 125tl, 127tr, 128tr, 132tc; Julius Shulman 9t; Harry Smith Collection 113br, 122bl, 126tl, 128tl, 131tl; Stephen J. Whitehorne 46–47

Key: t top, b bottom, l left, r right, c centre